Dominating Client
Fulfillment

Book 6

The Path to Prosperity Series

Strategic advisor Board
Achieve Systems Pro

ISBN: 978-1-957217-80-2 (hardcover)
ISBN: 978-1-957217-81-9 (paperback)
ISBN: 978-1-957217-82-6 (ebook)

TABLE OF CONTENTS

INTRODUCTION

THE IMPORTANCE OF FULFILLMENT IN MODERN BUSINESS

Fulfillment is one of those business terms we often hear, but it can sometimes seem a bit vague. Simply put, fulfillment is the process of getting a product from the seller to the customer. It covers everything from when an order is placed to when the customer receives their product. This includes handling the inventory, packing the items, and shipping them out. It's the behind-the-scenes work that makes sure customers get what they ordered when they expect it.

Fulfillment is crucial in the context of business. It's not just about moving products; it's about ensuring that the whole process runs smoothly. When fulfillment works well, customers are happy. They get their orders on time, in good condition, and without any hassle. This part of the business might not be glamorous, but it's vital. A seamless fulfillment process means fewer customer complaints, fewer returns, and better reviews.

Fulfillment plays a significant role in the customer journey, which is the customer's complete experience with a business from start to finish. Think of it as the backbone of customer satisfaction. When customers place an order, they start to build expectations. They expect their order to be processed quickly, shipped promptly, and delivered in perfect condition. Fulfillment is the mechanism that meets these expectations.

Let's say you're running an online store that sells custom t-shirts. When a customer places an order, they are eager to receive their unique shirt. They've already imagined wearing it and showing it off to their friends. If your fulfillment process is efficient, you'll confirm the order, pack the shirt carefully, and ship it out quickly. The customer receives the shirt just as they pictured it and is happy. This positive experience makes them more likely to order from you again and recommend your store to others.

On the other hand, if the fulfillment process is slow or the product arrives damaged, the customer's experience is ruined. They might not order from you again, and they could leave a bad review, which can harm your business's reputation. That's why good fulfillment is so important. It's about meeting and exceeding customer expectations.

In today's competitive market, efficient fulfillment can set your business apart. Customers have many options and often choose companies that deliver quickly and reliably. Focusing on your fulfillment process ensures that your customers are satisfied, which is key to building a loyal customer base and growing your business.

Efficient fulfillment processes play a huge role in customer satisfaction. When customers order something, they have certain expectations about how quickly and accurately they'll receive their purchase. If our fulfillment process is smooth, we meet those expectations, and customers are happy. They receive their orders on time, in good condition, and without any issues. This kind of reliability makes customers feel valued and respected.

Now, let's talk about the connection between fulfillment and customer loyalty. When customers are consistently satisfied with their orders, they start to trust our business. They know that they can count on us to deliver what we promise. This trust builds loyalty. Loyal customers are more likely to make repeat purchases and recommend us to others. It's a cycle that begins with efficient fulfillment. Companies like Amazon and Zappos are great examples. They have set high standards for fast, reliable delivery, and their customers keep coming back because they know they can depend on them.

Superior fulfillment can also give us a competitive edge. In a crowded market, anything that sets us apart is valuable. Exceptional fulfillment can be that differentiator. Customers notice when we consistently deliver faster and more reliably than our competitors. This edge can attract more customers and boost our market share. For instance, Warby Parker has gained a strong following not just because of their stylish glasses but also because of their efficient and customer-friendly fulfillment process. They make it easy for customers to try on glasses at home and return them if needed, which sets them apart from traditional eyewear retailers.

Operational efficiency and cost savings are other significant benefits of a streamlined fulfillment process. We can reduce errors and minimize returns by improving how we handle orders. This saves money on shipping, restocking, and customer service. Plus, it frees up resources that we can invest in other areas of the business. For example, by automating parts of our fulfillment process, we can handle more orders with the same amount of staff, reducing labor costs and increasing our capacity to grow. Companies like Ikea have mastered this, using highly efficient warehouses and inventory systems to keep costs low while maintaining high customer satisfaction.

Building a trustworthy brand hinges on reliable fulfillment. Our brand's reputation grows stronger when customers know they can count on us. This trust doesn't happen overnight; it's the result of consistently meeting or exceeding customer expectations over time. A strong brand reputation has long-term benefits, including increased customer loyalty and the ability to charge premium prices. Take Apple, for instance. Part of their brand trust comes from the reliability of their delivery and service processes, ensuring customers get their products promptly and in perfect condition.

Finally, the ability to adapt to market changes is crucial for any business. Agile fulfillment processes allow us to respond quickly to market fluctuations and changes in consumer demand. During the COVID-19 pandemic, many businesses had to pivot rapidly to online sales and home delivery. Those with flexible and efficient fulfillment systems could adapt more easily, meeting the surge in demand without compromising on service. Companies like Domino's Pizza quickly adjusted their fulfillment strategies to include no-contact delivery options, which helped them maintain customer trust and satisfaction during the crisis.

Efficient fulfillment isn't just about getting products from point A to point B. It's about creating a reliable, trustworthy experience that keeps customers happy and loyal, gives us a competitive edge, saves money, and helps us adapt to changes. When we get fulfillment right, it touches every part of our business in a positive way.

Overview of Physical and Digital Goods Fulfillment

Fulfillment is a critical part of running a business, whether we're dealing with physical or digital goods. Each type comes with its own set of steps and challenges. Understanding these processes can help us optimize our operations and improve customer satisfaction.

PHYSICAL GOODS FULFILLMENT

When it comes to physical goods, the fulfillment process starts with sourcing. Finding reliable suppliers who consistently provide quality products is essential. This means building relationships and negotiating terms that work for both parties. Once we have our products, we move on to inventory management. Keeping track of stock levels to ensure we can meet customer demand without overstocking is a delicate balance. Efficient inventory management helps prevent issues like stockouts and excess inventory, which can tie up capital.

Next, we need a good warehousing strategy. This involves choosing the right location, organizing the space efficiently, and ensuring that our products are stored safely. The goal is to make picking, packing, and shipping as smooth as possible. Logistics and shipping are the final steps. This includes choosing the best carriers, optimizing shipping routes, and handling returns efficiently. Each of these steps needs to work seamlessly to ensure that customers receive their orders on time and in good condition.

However, the fulfillment of physical goods isn't without challenges. Managing inventory can be complicated, especially as order volumes fluctuate. We might face delays from suppliers or issues with warehousing space. These challenges can disrupt the entire fulfillment process. Solutions often involve better planning, using technology to track inventory in real time, and having contingency plans for unexpected delays.

Technology plays a significant role in the fulfillment of physical goods. Inventory management systems help track stock levels and predict demand. Warehouse management systems optimize the storage and retrieval process. Logistics software helps plan the most efficient shipping routes and manage carrier relationships. Embracing technology can streamline operations and reduce errors, making the fulfillment process more efficient and reliable.

DIGITAL GOODS FULFILLMENT

For digital goods, the fulfillment process is different but equally important. It starts with order processing. When a customer makes a purchase, the system needs to handle the transaction quickly and securely. This involves verifying payment, generating an invoice, and updating records.

The next step is digital delivery. This could be sending an email with a download link, providing access to an online course, or enabling a software download. The key here is speed and reliability. Customers expect instant access to their digital purchases, and any delay can lead to dissatisfaction.

Digital goods fulfillment has its own set of benefits and challenges. On the plus side, there's no need for physical storage or shipping, which reduces overhead costs. However, ensuring secure and reliable delivery can be challenging. Technical issues can arise, and we need robust systems in place to handle them. Automation and technology are crucial in this area. Automated systems can process orders and deliver digital goods almost instantaneously. Using secure platforms ensures that digital products are delivered safely and without unauthorized access.

COMPARATIVE ANALYSIS

When comparing physical and digital goods fulfillment, several key differences stand out. Physical goods require more logistical planning, from inventory management to shipping. Digital goods, on the other hand, focus more on secure and instant delivery. Integrating these fulfillment processes can be challenging but rewarding for businesses that offer both types of products. It requires a flexible system that seamlessly handles physical logistics and digital delivery. Companies like Amazon excel at this, efficiently offering physical products and digital services.

INDUSTRY TRENDS

In terms of industry trends, both physical and digital fulfillment are evolving rapidly. For physical goods, trends include the use of robotics in warehouses, drone deliveries, and advanced logistics software. These technologies aim to make fulfillment faster and more efficient. For digital goods, trends include the use of blockchain for secure transactions, AI for personalized recommendations, and improved cybersecurity measures. We can expect these technologies to become even more integrated into fulfillment processes, offering new ways to enhance efficiency and customer satisfaction.

Understanding the fulfillment process for both physical and digital goods is essential for any business. By staying on top of industry trends and leveraging technology, we can ensure that our fulfillment processes are efficient, reliable, and capable of meeting customer expectations. This boosts customer satisfaction and gives us a competitive edge in the market.

PURPOSE AND GOALS OF THE BOOK

In writing this book, I aim to empower businesses to optimize their fulfillment processes. Fulfillment is often the backbone of a business, and mastering it can significantly improve efficiency, customer satisfaction, and profitability. I hope to help businesses streamline their operations and avoid common pitfalls by providing the necessary knowledge and tools. Throughout the book, you'll find case studies and practical examples illustrating key concepts and how other businesses have successfully implemented these strategies.

This book serves as a comprehensive guide to mastering fulfillment for both physical and digital goods. We'll cover every aspect, from sourcing products to providing excellent customer service. By breaking down each step in the fulfillment process, I aim to give you a clear understanding of what needs to be done and how to do it effectively. Whether you're handling inventory management, warehousing, or digital delivery, this guide offers detailed instructions to help you navigate the complexities of fulfillment.

One of the primary goals is to provide actionable strategies that you can implement immediately. These strategies are designed to be practical and easy to follow, ensuring you can start seeing improvements immediately. I've included checklists, templates, and best practices to make the implementation process as smooth as possible. These resources are meant to be used in your day-to-day operations, helping you to achieve better results without unnecessary complications.

Improving customer satisfaction is another key focus of this book. Effective fulfillment plays a crucial role in how customers perceive your business. You can enhance customer satisfaction and loyalty by delivering orders promptly and accurately. We'll explore tips for creating a customer-centric fulfillment process, ensuring that your customers have a positive experience every time they interact with your business. Happy customers are more likely to return and recommend your business to others, driving growth and success.

Boosting efficiency and reducing costs are also major themes. A streamlined fulfillment process can save significant costs by reducing errors, minimizing returns, and optimizing resources. Throughout the book, I'll highlight ways to make your operations more efficient, with examples of cost-saving measures that have worked for other businesses. By implementing these strategies, you can improve your bottom line while maintaining high standards of service.

Futureproofing your business is essential in today's fast-paced market. This book emphasizes the importance of adaptability and continuous improvement. We'll discuss how to prepare for future trends and challenges in fulfillment, ensuring that your business remains competitive and resilient. By staying ahead of the curve and embracing change, you can position your business for long-term success.

Encouraging ethical practices is another important goal. Sustainable and ethical fulfillment practices benefit the environment and build trust with customers. We'll explore examples of companies that have successfully implemented ethical practices, demonstrating how you can do the same. Promoting sustainability and ethical behavior can differentiate your business and appeal to a growing base of conscious consumers.

Finally, this book provides a clear roadmap for businesses to follow. Setting realistic goals and milestones is crucial for continuous improvement. I aim to give you a clear path forward by outlining a step-by-step plan. Whether you're looking to overhaul your entire fulfillment process or make incremental improvements, this roadmap will guide you every step of the way. By following the strategies and advice provided, you can transform your fulfillment process into a powerful asset for your business.

1

SETTING EXPECTATIONS

Setting expectations is one of the most crucial aspects of the fulfillment process. It's all about communication and clarity. When we set clear expectations, everyone knows what to expect and when to expect it. This not only smooths out our operations but also significantly enhances customer satisfaction.

Imagine placing an order online. You get a confirmation email that tells you exactly when your package will arrive and how you can track it. From that moment, you know what to expect. This clarity makes you feel confident in your purchase and satisfied with the service. The same principle applies to our business operations. When we communicate clearly with our customers and team, we set a standard everyone can follow.

Clear expectations also help prevent misunderstandings and disputes. When customers know the timeline for delivery and what steps to take if there's an issue, they're less likely to be upset if something goes wrong. They understand the process and feel more in control. This reduces the number of complaints and increases the chances of repeat business.

On the operational side, setting expectations ensures that our team is on the same page. Everyone understands their role and responsibilities, which helps avoid bottlenecks and delays. For example, if our warehouse team knows exactly when to expect new inventory and how quickly it needs to be processed, they can plan their work accordingly. This leads to a more efficient workflow and better use of resources.

IMPORTANCE OF SETTING CLEAR EXPECTATIONS

Setting clear expectations is vital for customer satisfaction. When customers know exactly what to expect from the moment they place an order, they feel more confident and assured. This clarity builds trust because it shows that we respect their time and value their business.

When we communicate clearly about order timelines, shipping details, and return policies, customers are less likely to experience unpleasant surprises. They know when their product will arrive, what to do if there's an issue, and how to get help if needed. This level of transparency makes customers feel taken care of and understood. It's a simple but powerful way to make sure they have a positive experience with our business.

Clear expectations also have a big impact on customer loyalty. Customers are more likely to come back when they are consistently satisfied with their experience. They remember how easy and predictable it was to buy from us, and that memory brings them back the next time they need something we offer. Over time, this trust builds a loyal customer base that returns and recommends us to others.

Moreover, setting expectations helps prevent misunderstandings and disputes. There is less room for confusion when customers are informed upfront about delivery times, potential delays, and our policies. If a delay happens, and the customer is already aware that this could be a possibility, they are more likely to be understanding. On the other hand, frustration sets in if they are expecting a quick delivery and there's a delay with no prior notice. Clear communication helps avoid these scenarios by keeping everyone on the same page.

INTERNAL PROCESSES AND STANDARDS

Having solid internal processes and standards for fulfillment is essential. These standards ensure that our operations run smoothly and that we deliver consistent, high-quality service to our customers. Developing these standards involves careful planning and attention to detail.

First, we need to define what our fulfillment process should look like. This means outlining every step, from receiving an order to shipping it out. We must think about handling inventory, packing items, and managing shipping logistics. By setting clear guidelines for each of these steps, we create a roadmap that everyone in the team can follow.

Training our staff to meet these standards is the next crucial step. It's not enough to simply tell them what the standards are; we need to ensure they understand them and can apply them consistently. This involves hands-on training, where we walk them through the process and explain why each step is important. Consistent training helps our team become proficient and confident in their roles, which in turn leads to a more efficient fulfillment process.

Documenting our processes and procedures is equally important. Written documentation serves as a reference that our team can consult whenever they need a reminder or clarification. It also ensures that new employees can quickly get up to speed. By having detailed documentation, we can maintain consistency even as our business grows or if we need to onboard new staff.

These internal processes and standards are the backbone of our fulfillment operations. They help us maintain high quality and efficiency, reduce errors, and improve overall customer satisfaction. By investing time in developing, training, and documenting these standards, we set ourselves up for long-term success. This structured approach makes our daily operations smoother and builds a strong foundation for future growth.

Communication with Customers

Communication with customers is key to ensuring a smooth fulfillment process. When customers know what to expect, it builds trust and satisfaction. It all starts with clearly communicating our fulfillment timelines and policies. We need to be upfront about how long it will take to process and ship an order and any specific shipping and return policies. This information should be easily accessible on our website, especially on product pages and during checkout.

Setting delivery expectations during checkout is crucial. As customers go through the process of placing their orders, we should provide clear information about estimated delivery times. This can be done by offering a range of dates based on their location and the shipping method they choose. Providing this information helps customers make informed decisions and reduces the likelihood of disappointment.

Once an order is placed, it's important to keep customers informed through confirmation emails and updates. The confirmation email should include all relevant details about the order, such as the items purchased, the total cost, and the estimated delivery date. This email reassures customers that their order has been received and is being processed.

As the order progresses, sending timely updates keeps customers in the loop. For example, an email confirming that the order has been shipped, along with tracking information, allows customers to follow their package's journey. If there are any delays or issues, it's better to communicate these as soon as possible rather than wait for the customer to reach out. By keeping communication clear and consistent, we can manage customer expectations effectively. This approach reduces the likelihood of complaints and enhances the overall customer experience. Customers appreciate being kept informed and are more likely to trust a business that communicates openly and transparently.

Clear communication with customers about fulfillment timelines and policies, setting delivery expectations during checkout, and providing regular updates are essential practices. These steps help build trust, reduce misunderstandings, and ensure a positive experience, which ultimately leads to higher customer satisfaction and loyalty.

HANDLING DELAYS AND ISSUES

Handling delays and issues is part of running a business, and how we communicate during these times makes all the difference. When delays happen, it's crucial to communicate with our customers promptly and transparently. This builds trust and shows that we value their time and business.

One of the best strategies is to be proactive. Instead of waiting for customers to reach out to us, we should notify them as soon as we know there's a delay. For example, if we find out that a shipment will be late, immediately sending an email or text message can prevent frustration. This message should explain the reason for the delay and provide an updated delivery estimate. Being upfront helps manage their expectations and shows that we're on top of the situation.

Proactive communication is generally more effective than reactive communication. When we wait for customers to come to us with their concerns, they're often already frustrated. By then, it's harder to turn the situation around. On the other hand, when we take the initiative, we can address their concerns before they escalate. This approach diffuses potential anger and demonstrates our commitment to customer service.

When communicating delays, it's also important to offer solutions. If a shipment is delayed, we might offer an expedited shipping option at no extra cost, a discount on their next purchase, or another form of compensation. This shows customers that we care about their experience and are willing to go the extra mile to make things right. Solutions like these can turn a negative situation into a positive one, often leaving customers more satisfied than if there had been no issue at all.

Managing customer dissatisfaction effectively requires empathy and action. When customers are upset, they want to feel heard and valued. Listening to their concerns without interrupting and acknowledging their frustration goes a long way. Once we understand their issue, we should apologize sincerely and provide a clear plan to resolve it. Whether it's replacing a damaged item or offering a refund, taking swift action shows that we stand by our products and services.

In summary, handling delays and issues with clear, proactive communication and offering practical solutions can maintain customer trust and satisfaction. By being transparent and empathetic, we can turn challenges into opportunities to strengthen our relationships with our customers.

Return and Refund Policies

Setting clear return and refund policies is essential for any business. These policies outline the process for customers to return products and receive refunds. They need to be straightforward and easy to understand. When customers know exactly what to expect if they need to return something, it builds confidence and trust in our business.

Communicating these policies to customers before they make a purchase is crucial. We should display our return and refund policies prominently on our website, especially on product pages and during checkout. This transparency helps customers make informed decisions and reduces the likelihood of surprises or frustrations later on. When customers can easily find and understand our policies, it reassures them that we stand behind our products and are committed to their satisfaction.

Once a customer decides to return a product, handling the return and refund process smoothly is key to maintaining their trust. We need to make the process as simple and hassle-free as possible. Providing clear return instructions, such as how to package the item and where to send it, helps streamline the process. Promptly processing refunds once we receive the returned item is also important. Customers appreciate quick resolutions, and it shows that we value their time and business.

We can enhance customer satisfaction and loyalty by ensuring that our return and refund policies are clear, well-communicated, and efficiently executed. This approach helps resolve issues and demonstrates our commitment to providing a positive shopping experience. Trust is built through these consistent, transparent interactions, making customers more likely to return and recommend our business to others.

TOOLS AND TECHNOLOGIES FOR MANAGING EXPECTATIONS

Using the right tools and technologies can make a big difference in managing customer expectations. These tools help us communicate clearly and efficiently, which is crucial for keeping our customers happy.

One of the most valuable tools for this purpose is a Customer Relationship Management (CRM) system. A good

CRM system allows us to track all our customer interactions. This helps us remember important details about their preferences and past orders so we can provide more personalized service. With a CRM, we can also automate follow-up emails and notifications, ensuring that customers are always informed about the status of their orders.

Order tracking software is another essential tool. By integrating this software with our online store, we can provide customers with real-time updates on their shipments. Customers can see exactly where their order is and when it is expected to arrive. This transparency builds trust and reduces the number of inquiries we receive about order statuses.

Technology also allows us to automate many aspects of our communication with customers. For example, we can set up automated emails to confirm orders, notify customers when their items have shipped, and provide delivery updates. These automated messages ensure that customers receive timely information without us having to manually send each email. This not only saves time but also ensures consistency in our communications.

Additionally, our website's chatbots and live chat features can provide immediate answers to common questions. Customers appreciate quick responses, and these tools can handle inquiries 24/7, improving their overall experience with our business.

By leveraging these technologies, we can streamline our communication processes and provide customers with the information they need when they need it. This helps set and manage their expectations effectively, leading to higher satisfaction and a smoother fulfillment process. Keeping our customers informed and engaged with the help of these tools ultimately strengthens our relationships with them and enhances their trust in our business.

Continuous Improvement

Continuous improvement is essential for any business that wants to stay competitive and meet the evolving needs of its customers. Regularly reviewing and updating our expectations and communication strategies ensures that we keep pace with changes in the market and continue to meet customer expectations.

Gathering customer feedback is one of the most effective ways to drive improvement. Feedback is invaluable because it provides direct insights into what we're doing well and where we need to improve. By asking our customers about their experiences, we can identify patterns and common issues that might not be apparent from an internal perspective. This can be done through surveys, reviews, or even casual conversations.

Once we have this feedback, it's important to take action. This means analyzing the feedback to understand the underlying issues and then implementing changes to address them. For example, if customers frequently mention delays in delivery, we might need to look at our shipping processes and find ways to expedite them. Performance metrics, such as delivery times, return rates, and customer satisfaction scores, can also help us pinpoint areas for improvement.

Implementing changes based on feedback and performance metrics isn't just about fixing problems. It's also about making good processes even better. Continuous improvement means always looking for ways to enhance efficiency, reduce costs, and provide a better customer experience. This could involve adopting new technologies, refining our workflows, or offering additional training to our staff.

Committing to continuous improvement demonstrates to our customers that we value their input and are dedicated to providing the best possible service. It builds trust and loyalty as customers see that we're proactive in addressing their concerns and constantly striving to exceed their expectations. This ongoing feedback and improvement process helps us stay ahead of the competition and keeps our business moving forward.

Conclusion

In conclusion, setting clear expectations in the fulfillment process is crucial for any business aiming to build a strong, loyal customer base. By clearly communicating what customers can expect in terms of delivery times, return policies, and overall service, we create a foundation of trust and reliability. This transparency is key to ensuring that customers feel valued and informed throughout their entire experience with our business.

Clear expectations enhance customer satisfaction by reducing the likelihood of misunderstandings and disappointments. When customers know exactly what to expect, they are more likely to feel positive about their purchase and the service they receive. This leads to repeat business and positive word-of-mouth, both of which are essential for growth.

On the operational side, clear expectations streamline our processes and improve efficiency. When everyone on our team understands the standards and procedures, it reduces errors and delays. This not only saves time and money but also helps maintain a high level of service quality. Efficient operations mean we can handle more orders smoothly, keeping our customers happy and our business running effectively.

Setting and managing expectations is about aligning our promises with our capabilities. It's about being honest and proactive in our communications, ensuring that our customers and team are on the same page. By doing so, we can build a stronger, more efficient business that consistently meets and exceeds customer expectations. This commitment to clarity and transparency will serve as a cornerstone for ongoing success and customer loyalty.

2

SOURCING QUALITY PRODUCTS

Sourcing quality products is one of the most critical aspects of running a successful business. It's about finding reliable suppliers who provide goods that consistently meet our standards. The quality of the products we source affects everything from our inventory management to customer satisfaction. When we source high-quality products, we reduce the risk of returns and complaints, streamline our operations, and build a stronger reputation with our customers.

The impact of sourcing on the fulfillment process is significant. High-quality products mean fewer defects, which translates to fewer returns and less hassle for both us and our customers. It ensures that customers are pleased with what they get when they receive their orders, leading to higher satisfaction and repeat business. Consistency in product quality also means that our fulfillment team can operate more efficiently without constantly dealing with quality issues or unexpected problems.

This chapter will explore several key areas related to sourcing quality products. First, we'll discuss identifying and selecting reliable suppliers who consistently deliver the quality we need. This involves evaluating potential suppliers and establishing strong relationships. Next, we'll look at negotiating contracts and terms to ensure we get the best value without compromising quality. We will also delve into the importance of ethical and sustainable sourcing as more consumers demand transparency and responsibility from the brands they support.

We'll cover the implementation of quality control measures to maintain high standards and handle any issues that arise. Cost management is another crucial topic; we'll explore how to balance cost and quality effectively. Maintaining good supplier relationships is vital, and we'll discuss communication and conflict resolution strategies. Real-world examples and case studies will provide practical insights and lessons learned from successful businesses. Finally, we'll touch on future trends in sourcing, including the role of technology and emerging practices in ethical and sustainable sourcing.

By the end of this chapter, you'll have a comprehensive understanding of the importance of sourcing quality products and practical strategies to ensure your business excels in this area.

Understanding Quality in Sourcing

Understanding quality in sourcing is essential for running a successful business. When we talk about quality products, we are referring to items that meet specific standards of performance, durability, and appearance. These products should perform their intended function effectively and reliably. They should also be durable, meaning they last as expected without breaking down or deteriorating quickly. Finally, they should look good, as aesthetics can often be just as important as functionality, especially in competitive markets.

Consistency in product quality is crucial. Customers expect the same level of quality every time they purchase from us. If the quality fluctuates, it can lead to dissatisfaction and a lack of trust. Consistent quality ensures that customers know exactly what they are getting, which builds confidence in our brand. When a product meets or exceeds expectations every time, customers are more likely to return and recommend us to others. This consistency is a cornerstone of customer loyalty.

The impact of product quality on our brand reputation cannot be overstated. High-quality products enhance our brand image and establish us as a reliable and trustworthy business. When customers know they can count on our products to be of high quality, they are more likely to develop a positive perception of our brand. This positive reputation spreads through word-of-mouth and reviews, attracting more customers and driving growth.

On the flip side, poor product quality can severely damage our reputation. Customers who receive subpar products will likely be dissatisfied and vocal about their negative experiences. This can lead to bad reviews, returns, and a tarnished brand image. Recovering from such damage can be difficult and costly. Therefore, maintaining high standards of quality is not just about satisfying customers today but also about securing the long-term health of our business.

In summary, understanding what constitutes a quality product and ensuring consistency in that quality are fundamental to building and maintaining a strong brand. High-quality products foster customer loyalty and enhance our reputation, which are critical components of sustainable business success. Focusing on quality in our sourcing can create a solid foundation for growth and customer satisfaction.

IDENTIFYING RELIABLE SUPPLIERS

Identifying reliable suppliers is crucial for maintaining high standards in our business. To find the right partners, we need to establish clear criteria. Reliable suppliers should consistently deliver products that meet our quality standards. They should have a proven track record, demonstrated through their ability to meet deadlines and provide excellent customer service. Financial stability is another key factor. Financially sound suppliers are less likely to face issues that could disrupt their operations and, by extension, ours.

Building strong relationships with our suppliers plays a significant role in ensuring product quality. A good supplier relationship is built on trust and open communication. When we establish a strong rapport with our suppliers, it becomes easier to address any issues that arise and work collaboratively to find solutions. Regular communication helps us stay informed about any potential changes or challenges that could impact the supply chain. These relationships are a two-way street; just as we rely on our suppliers, they also depend on us for consistent orders and clear communication.

Evaluating potential suppliers requires a thorough approach. Site visits allow us to see their operations firsthand and assess their capacity and processes. During these visits, we can observe their production methods, quality control measures, and overall efficiency. References from other businesses can provide insights into the supplier's reliability and performance. Additionally, requesting samples is a practical way to test the quality of their products before committing to a larger order. These steps help ensure we choose suppliers who consistently meet our standards.

Diversifying our supplier base is also important for mitigating risk. Relying on a single supplier can be risky if they encounter problems or cannot meet our demands. Having multiple suppliers ensures continuity in our supply chain, even if one supplier faces issues. This diversity also allows us to compare suppliers and negotiate better terms, benefiting our business.

Negotiating Contracts and Terms

Negotiating contracts and terms with suppliers is crucial to sourcing quality products. A good contract sets the foundation for a strong business relationship, ensuring that both parties understand their responsibilities and expectations. Key elements of a supplier contract include the specifics of the product, delivery schedules, payment terms, and quality standards. It's essential to be detailed in these areas to avoid any misunderstandings later on.

When negotiating terms, it's important to strike a balance between favorable conditions and maintaining quality. While we want to get the best possible deal, we also need to ensure that the supplier can meet our quality standards. This means being realistic about costs and timelines. If a price seems too good to be true, it might be because the supplier is cutting corners somewhere. Effectively negotiating involves understanding the supplier's costs and finding a fair price that benefits both parties.

Setting clear expectations and standards in the contract is another critical aspect. This includes specifying the quality of the products, the inspection and testing processes, and the consequences if standards are not met. By being explicit about these details, we can ensure that the supplier knows exactly what is required and what will happen if there are issues. This clarity helps prevent disputes and ensures that both parties are aligned from the start.

Building long-term partnerships with suppliers requires more than just a good contract. It involves ongoing communication and collaboration. Regularly reviewing the performance of our suppliers and providing feedback helps build trust and improve the relationship. It's also beneficial to be flexible and understanding when issues arise, as long as they are handled transparently and promptly. By fostering a positive relationship, we create a partnership where both parties are invested in each other's success.

In summary, negotiating contracts and terms involves creating detailed agreements, balancing favorable conditions with quality, setting clear standards, and fostering long-term partnerships. These steps ensure that we can maintain high standards for our products while building strong, mutually beneficial relationships with our suppliers. By approaching negotiations with a focus on fairness and collaboration, we can secure reliable sources for our quality products.

ETHICAL AND SUSTAINABLE SOURCING

Ethical and sustainable sourcing is becoming increasingly important in today's business environment. More and more customers are looking for brands that deliver quality products and care about their impact on the world. Focusing on sustainability shows our commitment to responsible business practices, which can set us apart from our competitors and build stronger connections with our customers.

Ensuring that our suppliers adhere to ethical practices starts with setting clear standards. We must establish guidelines covering everything from labor practices to environmental impact. This means choosing suppliers who treat their workers fairly, provide safe working conditions, and follow environmental regulations. Regular audits and inspections are necessary to ensure compliance. Visiting suppliers, reviewing their practices, and even talking to workers can give us a clear picture of how they operate.

The benefits of sustainable sourcing are significant for both our brand and the environment. From a business perspective, it can enhance our reputation and attract customers who value sustainability. It also helps build long-term relationships with suppliers who are committed to the same values. Environmentally, sustainable practices reduce waste, conserve resources, and minimize our carbon footprint. This not only helps protect the planet but also ensures that we are contributing to a better future.

Several companies excel in ethical sourcing, setting examples for the rest of us. For instance, Patagonia is well-known for its commitment to sustainability. They go to great lengths to ensure their products are made ethically, using environmentally friendly materials and working with suppliers who adhere to strict ethical standards. Another example is IKEA, which has made significant strides in sustainable sourcing by using renewable materials and investing in sustainable forestry.

Focusing on ethical and sustainable sourcing is essential for modern businesses. It not only enhances our brand and attracts conscious consumers but also contributes to the well-being of our planet. By setting clear standards, ensuring compliance, and learning from leaders in the field, we can make a positive impact and build a more sustainable future.

QUALITY CONTROL MEASURES

Implementing quality control measures with suppliers is crucial for maintaining the high standards that our customers expect. It begins with setting up clear processes that outline how products should be tested and evaluated before they reach us. This means working closely with suppliers to establish these procedures and ensuring that they have the resources and knowledge to carry them out effectively.

Regular audits and inspections are a key part of this process. By periodically reviewing our suppliers' operations, we can ensure that they continue to meet our standards. These audits might involve visiting their facilities, reviewing their quality control processes, and even conducting surprise inspections. This helps us catch any potential issues early and address them before they impact our customers. It's not just about finding problems but also about working with suppliers to improve their practices.

When quality issues or defects arise, handling them promptly and efficiently is important. We need to have a clear process in place for addressing these problems, which includes identifying the root cause, finding a solution, and preventing future occurrences. This might involve working closely with the supplier to adjust their processes or providing additional training and support. The goal is to ensure the issue is resolved and our quality standards are maintained.

Technology plays a significant role in enhancing quality control. Advanced software and tools can help us track and monitor quality throughout the supply chain. For example, using digital tracking systems allows us to keep detailed records of each batch of products, making it easier to trace any issues back to their source. Automated testing equipment can also provide more consistent and accurate results than manual inspections.

In conclusion, quality control measures are essential for ensuring that our products meet the standards our customers expect. By implementing clear processes, conducting regular audits, addressing issues promptly, and leveraging technology, we can maintain high-quality standards and build stronger relationships with our suppliers. This commitment to quality protects our brand and ensures that our customers receive the best possible products.

Cost Management in Sourcing

Managing costs in sourcing is a delicate balancing act. On one hand, we need to keep our expenses in check to maintain profitability. On the other, we can't afford to compromise on quality, as that would hurt our brand and customer satisfaction. The key is finding that sweet spot where cost and quality meet harmoniously.

One effective strategy for reducing costs without sacrificing quality is building strong relationships with suppliers. We can often negotiate better terms and prices by working closely with them. For example, suppliers might offer discounts if we commit to larger orders or longer contracts. This approach helps us save money and ensures a consistent supply of high-quality products.

Bulk purchasing is another way to manage costs. We often secure lower prices per unit when we buy in larger quantities. This is especially beneficial for items that we know will sell steadily over time. However, it's important to plan carefully to avoid overstocking, which can tie up capital and lead to storage issues. Long-term contracts can also provide cost benefits by locking in prices and terms for an extended period, protecting us from market fluctuations.

Managing financial risks, such as currency fluctuations, is another crucial aspect of cost management. When sourcing from international suppliers, changes in exchange rates can significantly impact our costs. We might use financial instruments like forward contracts to lock in exchange rates or work with suppliers to agree on pricing in a stable currency to mitigate this risk. This helps us maintain predictable costs and avoid unexpected financial hits.

In summary, cost management in sourcing involves a careful balance between maintaining quality and controlling expenses. By leveraging strong supplier relationships, bulk purchasing, and long-term contracts and managing financial risks, we can keep our costs down without compromising the quality our customers expect. This strategic approach ensures that we remain competitive and profitable while delivering the high standards for which our brand is known.

SUPPLIER RELATIONSHIP MANAGEMENT

Maintaining good relationships with our suppliers is crucial for the success of our business. These relationships are the backbone of our supply chain, ensuring we receive quality products on time. Good supplier relationships lead to better pricing, more reliable deliveries, and often, preferential treatment when supplies are tight. Suppliers who trust us and feel valued are more likely to go the extra mile to meet our needs, which in turn helps us keep our customers happy.

Effective communication is key to managing these relationships. Regular, open, and honest communication helps build trust and ensures that both parties are on the same page. Whether it's discussing delivery schedules, quality expectations, or addressing any issues that arise, clear communication helps avoid misunderstandings and keeps things running smoothly. Scheduling regular check-ins through phone calls, video conferences, or in-person meetings helps maintain a strong connection and allows us to promptly address any concerns.

Disputes and conflicts with suppliers are inevitable, but how we handle them can make all the difference. It's important to approach these situations with a problem-solving mindset rather than a confrontational one. By focusing on finding a mutually beneficial solution, we can often resolve conflicts in a way that strengthens the relationship. It's also helpful to have clear processes in place for handling disputes, which can provide a roadmap for resolution and ensure that both parties know what to expect.

Collaboration with suppliers is essential for continuous improvement. By working together, we can identify areas for improvement and develop strategies to address them. This might involve sharing data and insights, co-developing new products, or jointly working on process improvements. Collaboration fosters innovation and helps both parties achieve their goals more efficiently. When suppliers see that we are invested in their success, they are more likely to be invested in ours.

Supplier relationship management is about building strong, trust-based relationships through effective communication, proactive dispute resolution, and ongoing collaboration. These efforts ensure that our supply chain is robust and reliable, which in turn supports our overall business success. We create a foundation for long-term success and continuous improvement by valuing and nurturing our supplier relationships.

FUTURE TRENDS IN SOURCING

Future trends in sourcing are evolving rapidly, and staying ahead of these changes is crucial for maintaining a competitive edge. One of the most significant global sourcing and supply chain management trends is the shift toward more agile and resilient supply chains. Businesses are increasingly diversifying their supplier bases to reduce dependency on any single source and to mitigate risks. This approach enhances supply chain resilience and allows businesses to respond more swiftly to market changes and disruptions.

Technology is playing a transformative role in sourcing. Artificial intelligence (AI) is revolutionizing how we predict demand, manage inventory, and optimize logistics. AI-driven analytics provide deeper insights into market trends and supplier performance, enabling more informed decision-making. Blockchain technology is another game-changer, offering unprecedented transparency and traceability in the supply chain. By securely recording every transaction, blockchain helps prevent fraud, ensures compliance, and builds trust among all parties involved. Automation is streamlining many sourcing processes, from order management to quality control, reducing human error and increasing efficiency.

The future of ethical and sustainable sourcing looks promising as well. Consumers are more aware of and concerned about the ethical implications of their purchases, driving businesses to adopt more sustainable practices. We can expect to see a greater emphasis on sourcing environmentally friendly materials produced under fair labor conditions. Companies are likely to invest more in green technologies and sustainable supply chain practices, such as reducing carbon footprints and waste.

As we look ahead, it's clear that technology will continue to shape the sourcing landscape. Businesses that embrace AI, blockchain, and automation will have a significant advantage. Furthermore, the push for ethical and sustainable sourcing will become more pronounced, with businesses striving to meet the growing consumer demand for transparency and responsibility. By staying informed about these trends and integrating them into our sourcing strategies, we can ensure that our business remains competitive, resilient, and aligned with the values of our customers. This forward-thinking approach will help us navigate the complexities of the modern supply chain and thrive in an ever-changing market.

CONCLUSION

In conclusion, sourcing quality products is essential for the success and sustainability of our business. Throughout this chapter, we have discussed various aspects of sourcing, from identifying reliable suppliers and negotiating favorable contracts to implementing quality control measures and managing costs effectively. We also explored the significance of ethical and sustainable sourcing and examined the latest trends that are shaping the future of our industry.

Sourcing quality products is more than just a business necessity; it is a commitment to our customers and our brand. High-quality products enhance customer satisfaction and build loyalty, which in turn drives repeat business and positive word-of-mouth. Reliable suppliers and strong supplier relationships are the foundation of this commitment, ensuring that we can consistently deliver the products our customers expect.

It's important to remember that sourcing is not a one-time effort but an ongoing process. Markets change, new technologies emerge, and customer expectations evolve. We must continuously evaluate and improve our sourcing practices to stay competitive and responsive to these changes. This means staying informed about industry trends, regularly reviewing supplier performance, and being proactive in addressing any issues that arise.

We can build a resilient and efficient supply chain that supports our long-term business goals by prioritizing quality in our sourcing strategies and being open to continuous improvement. This proactive approach will help us navigate challenges, seize new opportunities, and ultimately deliver exceptional value to our customers. Let's commit to sourcing with integrity and excellence, ensuring that our products stand out in the market and our business thrives.

3

INVENTORY MANAGEMENT FOR PHYSICAL GOODS

Inventory management is a critical aspect of running a successful business. It involves overseeing the flow of goods from suppliers to our warehouse and, ultimately, to our customers. Effective inventory management ensures that we have the right products in the right quantities at the right time. This balance is essential to meet customer demand without overstocking or understocking, both of which can have significant financial impacts.

The importance of inventory management in the supply chain cannot be overstated. It directly affects our ability to fulfill orders promptly and accurately, which in turn influences customer satisfaction and loyalty. When inventory is managed well, we can reduce costs associated with holding and storing products, minimize losses due to obsolescence or spoilage, and improve cash flow. Moreover, it enables us to react swiftly to market changes and customer needs, giving us a competitive edge.

Effective inventory management contributes to overall business success by streamlining operations and enhancing efficiency. It helps us avoid the pitfalls of excess inventory, such as tied-up capital and increased storage costs, while also preventing stockouts that can lead to missed sales opportunities and disappointed customers. A well-organized inventory system also facilitates better decision-making by providing accurate stock level data, turnover rate, and demand patterns.

In this chapter, we will explore several key areas of inventory management for physical goods. We will begin with understanding what inventory management entails and the various types of inventory we need to manage. We will then discuss different inventory management techniques, such as Just-in-Time (JIT), Economic Order Quantity (EOQ), and ABC analysis, which can help us optimize our inventory levels. The role of inventory control systems, including both manual and automated options, will also be covered, highlighting how technology can enhance our inventory processes.

Demand forecasting will be another focal point, as accurate predictions of customer demand are crucial for maintaining optimal inventory levels. We will look at how to calculate and interpret the inventory turnover ratio, a key metric for assessing our inventory efficiency. Warehouse management practices, including layout design and the use of warehouse management systems (WMS), will also be discussed to ensure that our storage and retrieval processes are as efficient as possible.

Regular inventory audits and reconciliation are necessary to maintain accurate records and identify discrepancies. We will explore methods for conducting these audits and how to address any issues that arise. Additionally, we will delve into inventory optimization techniques to balance stock levels with demand while minimizing costs.

Finally, this chapter will include real-world examples and case studies to illustrate successful inventory management strategies and look at future trends and technologies shaping the field. By understanding and implementing the principles of effective inventory management, we can enhance our operational efficiency, reduce costs, and improve overall business performance.

Understanding Inventory Management

Inventory management is all about keeping track of the goods we have and making sure we have enough stock to meet customer demand without overdoing it. It's like a balancing act, ensuring we don't run out of popular products while avoiding excess stock that ties up our cash. The purpose of inventory management is to maintain the right amount of inventory at all times, which helps us meet customer needs promptly and efficiently.

Effective inventory management plays a crucial role in meeting customer demand. When we have the right products available at the right time, our customers are happy, and their satisfaction grows. This, in turn, builds loyalty and encourages repeat business. For instance, if a customer orders a product, they expect it to be in stock and delivered on time. Good inventory management ensures that we can fulfill these orders without delays, maintaining a smooth and reliable service.

Moreover, inventory management is key to controlling costs. Holding too much inventory ties up our capital and increases storage costs, while having too little can lead to stockouts and missed sales opportunities. By carefully managing our inventory, we can minimize these costs, ensuring we're not spending more than necessary on storage and handling. This balance helps us maintain a healthy profit margin and stay competitive in the market.

Overall, inventory management isn't just about keeping track of stock. It's a strategic function that impacts our entire supply chain, from sourcing and warehousing to order fulfillment and customer satisfaction. By understanding its importance, we can implement better practices and systems, making our business more efficient and responsive to customer needs.

TYPES OF INVENTORY

When managing inventory, it's important to understand the different types of inventory we deal with. Each type plays a unique role in our operations and requires specific strategies for effective management.

Raw materials are the basic inputs used in the production of our goods. These are the building blocks of what we create and sell. Managing raw materials involves ensuring we have enough stock to keep production running smoothly without overstocking and tying up too much capital. For example, if we manufacture furniture, raw materials would include wood, screws, nails, and varnish. Keeping an optimal level of raw materials helps prevent production delays and keeps our costs in check.

Work-in-progress (WIP) refers to items that are in the middle of the production process. These are products that have started being worked on but are not yet finished. Managing WIP inventory is crucial for maintaining a steady production flow. Too much WIP can indicate bottlenecks in our process, while too little might mean we're not utilizing our production capacity efficiently. For instance, in a furniture factory, a partially assembled chair is WIP. Tracking WIP helps us identify and resolve inefficiencies in our production line.

Finished goods are the products that are ready for sale. This is the inventory that directly impacts our sales and revenue. Effective management of finished goods ensures that we can meet customer demand promptly. If our finished goods inventory is too high, it means we have excess stock that could become obsolete or incur additional storage costs. On the other hand, if it's too low, we risk stockouts and missed sales.

For example, having a warehouse full of ready-to-ship furniture ensures we can fulfill customer orders quickly, boosting satisfaction and loyalty.

Maintenance, repair, and operations (MRO) supplies are items used to support the production process but are not part of the final product. These include things like lubricants for machinery, cleaning supplies, and tools. While they may not seem as critical as raw materials or finished goods, managing MRO inventory is essential for minimizing downtime and maintaining smooth operations. For instance, running out of a crucial cleaning solvent for our machinery can halt production, leading to delays and increased costs.

Understanding the different types of inventory—raw materials, WIP, finished goods, and MRO supplies—helps us develop tailored strategies for each category. This ensures a balanced and efficient inventory management system that supports our overall business goals and keeps our operations running smoothly.

INVENTORY MANAGEMENT TECHNIQUES

Effective inventory management is crucial for maintaining smooth operations and ensuring customer satisfaction. We can use several techniques to manage our inventory effectively, each with its own set of benefits and challenges.

One popular method is Just-in-Time (JIT) inventory. The idea behind JIT is to keep inventory levels as low as possible, only ordering goods as they are needed for production or sales. This approach can significantly reduce storage costs and minimize waste. However, it also requires a highly reliable supply chain. If there are any delays from suppliers, it can lead to production stoppages and unhappy customers. For example, in a furniture business, JIT means ordering wood and screws only when we receive an order for a new piece of furniture, ensuring we don't have large quantities of materials sitting unused.

Another technique is Economic Order Quantity (EOQ). EOQ is a formula used to determine the optimal order quantity that minimizes the total inventory cost, including holding and ordering costs. By calculating EOQ, we can find the sweet spot where the costs are balanced. This involves some math, but the idea is to order just enough inventory to meet demand without overstocking. For example, if our furniture business calculates that ordering 100 units of wood at a time is most cost-effective, we would stick to that amount to minimize our costs.

ABC Analysis is another useful tool for managing inventory. This technique involves categorizing inventory into three groups: A, B, and C. 'A' items are the most valuable and require the most attention, 'B' items are important but not as critical, and 'C' items are the least valuable. By focusing our efforts on the 'A' items, we can ensure that the most important products are always available. In our furniture business, expensive hardwoods might be 'A' items, mid-range materials might be 'B,' and inexpensive supplies like nails might be 'C.'

Safety stock is also a critical component of inventory management. This is the extra inventory kept on hand to prevent stockouts in case of unexpected demand or supply chain disruptions. Safety stock acts as a buffer, ensuring that we can continue to meet customer demands even if there are delays in replenishment. Calculating the right amount of safety stock involves considering factors like lead time and variability in demand. For instance, if our varnish supplier is known for occasional delays, we might keep extra varnish on hand to ensure we can still complete our furniture orders on time.

Inventory Control Systems

Effectively managing inventory means deciding between manual and automated control systems. Manual inventory control involves physically counting stock and keeping records by hand or in spreadsheets. This method can work for small businesses with limited inventory but becomes increasingly cumbersome and error prone as the business grows. Mistakes in counting or data entry can lead to inaccurate stock levels, disrupting operations and customer dissatisfaction.

On the other hand, automated inventory control systems use technology to track and manage inventory. Implementing barcode and RFID systems can significantly streamline this process. Barcodes and RFID tags allow us to quickly scan items in and out of inventory, providing real-time updates on stock levels. This reduces the chance of human error and saves a tremendous amount of time compared to manual counting. For example, scanning barcodes as we receive shipments or sell items in our furniture business ensures our inventory records are always up to date.

Using inventory management software adds another layer of efficiency. These software systems can automatically track inventory levels, generate reordering alerts, and provide detailed reports on stock movements. This kind of software helps us make informed decisions about purchasing and inventory management. For instance, if the software alerts us that our stock of a particular type of wood is running low, we can reorder before we run out, avoiding production delays.

Integration with other business systems like ERP (Enterprise Resource Planning) and CRM (Customer Relationship Management) systems is also crucial. By linking our inventory management system with ERP, we can synchronize inventory data with our financial and operational systems, providing a comprehensive view of our business performance. Integration with CRM systems allows us to better understand customer demand and adjust our inventory levels accordingly. For example, suppose our CRM shows an increase in customer interest for a new furniture design. In that case, our inventory system can help ensure we have enough materials on hand to meet this demand.

While manual inventory control can be suitable for very small operations, automated systems offer significant advantages in terms of accuracy, efficiency, and scalability. Implementing barcode and RFID systems, using inventory management software, and integrating with other business systems help us maintain optimal inventory levels, reduce costs, and improve overall business operations. By leveraging these technologies, we can focus more on growing our business and less on managing inventory issues.

DEMAND FORECASTING

Accurate demand forecasting is crucial for managing our inventory effectively. By predicting customer demand, we can ensure that we have the right amount of stock on hand, avoiding both overstocking and stockouts. This balance is essential for maintaining customer satisfaction and keeping costs under control.

One of the key techniques for forecasting demand is analyzing historical data. We can identify patterns and trends that help us predict future demand by looking at past sales. For instance, if we notice that a particular type of furniture consistently sells well during the holiday season, we can prepare by increasing our stock ahead of time. This approach helps us make informed decisions based on actual sales data, reducing the guesswork involved in inventory management.

Market trends and seasonality also play a significant role in demand forecasting. Understanding broader market trends allows us to anticipate changes in customer preferences and adjust our inventory accordingly. For example, if there is a growing trend toward eco-friendly furniture, we can increase our stock of products made from sustainable materials. Seasonality, such as higher demand for outdoor furniture in the summer, also affects our inventory management. By recognizing these patterns, we can better align our stock levels with expected demand.

Collaborative planning with suppliers and customers is another effective technique for demand forecasting. By working closely with our suppliers, we can gain insights into potential supply chain disruptions or opportunities, allowing us to adjust our inventory plans accordingly. Similarly, engaging with our customers helps us understand their needs and preferences, providing valuable information for our forecasting efforts. For instance, if a key customer indicates they plan to place a large order next quarter, we can ensure we have the necessary stock to meet their needs.

In summary, accurate demand forecasting is vital for effective inventory management. Techniques such as historical data analysis, understanding market trends and seasonality, and collaborative planning with suppliers and customers all contribute to making more accurate predictions. By leveraging these methods, we can maintain optimal inventory levels, reduce costs, and enhance customer satisfaction, ultimately driving the success of our business.

INVENTORY TURNOVER RATIO

The inventory turnover ratio is crucial for understanding how efficiently we manage our stock. This ratio measures how often our inventory is sold and replaced over a specific period. A high turnover rate indicates that we are selling our products quickly and not holding on to excess inventory, which is ideal.

Conversely, a low turnover rate can signal overstocking or slow-moving inventory, which ties up capital and increases storage costs.

To calculate the inventory turnover ratio, we divide the cost of goods sold (COGS) by the average inventory for the period. For example, if our COGS for the year is $500,000 and our average inventory is $100,000, our inventory turnover ratio is 5. This means we turned over our inventory five times during the year. This calculation gives us a clear picture of how efficiently we're managing our stock levels.

Interpreting the inventory turnover ratio involves looking at the context of our specific industry and business model. A higher ratio generally means better performance, but it must be balanced against the need to meet customer demand without frequent stockouts. For instance, if our turnover ratio is much higher than the industry average, it could mean we're not keeping enough inventory on hand, leading to lost sales opportunities. On the other hand, a significantly lower ratio might indicate overstocking, which can lead to increased holding costs and obsolete inventory.

Improving our inventory turnover involves several strategies. One effective approach is to refine our demand forecasting. By accurately predicting customer demand, we can better align our inventory levels with actual sales, reducing excess stock and avoiding stockouts. Another strategy is to optimize our inventory management practices, such as implementing just-in-time (JIT) inventory systems to minimize holding costs. Regularly reviewing our product mix and discontinuing slow-moving items can also help improve our turnover rate.

Moreover, enhancing our sales and marketing efforts can drive demand and boost turnover. Promoting products through targeted campaigns, offering discounts or incentives for bulk purchases, and improving our online presence can all contribute to higher sales and faster inventory turnover.

The inventory turnover ratio is a vital measure of our inventory management efficiency. We can gain valuable insights into our stock management practices by calculating and interpreting this ratio. Implementing strategies to improve our turnover ratio, such as better demand forecasting, optimized inventory practices, and enhanced sales efforts, will help us maintain the right balance of inventory, reduce costs, and meet customer demand more effectively.

Warehouse Management

Warehouse management is a key component of running a successful business. It involves everything from how we design our warehouse layout to the systems we use to track our inventory. An efficient warehouse layout and design can significantly affect how smoothly our operations run. The goal is to optimize space and streamline workflows, ensuring products move quickly and efficiently from receiving to storage to shipping.

When designing a warehouse layout, we need to consider the flow of goods. Products should move in a logical sequence from receiving to storage to picking and finally to shipping. This reduces unnecessary movement and handling, saving time and reducing the risk of errors. For example, placing high-demand items closer to the shipping area can speed up the picking process. Similarly, grouping similar items together can make it easier for workers to locate and pick them.

Best practices for receiving, storing, and picking inventory are crucial in warehouse management. It's important to check shipments against purchase orders to ensure accuracy when receiving inventory. Any discrepancies should be addressed immediately to avoid issues later. Proper storage techniques, such as using racks and shelves efficiently and labeling everything clearly, help keep the warehouse organized and make it easier to find items. The picking process should be streamlined, with clear instructions and efficient routes to minimize time and effort.

Implementing a warehouse management system (WMS) can greatly enhance our warehouse operations. A WMS helps track inventory in real time, manage stock levels, and optimize storage and picking processes. It provides visibility into what's in the warehouse, where it's located, and when it needs to be replenished. This reduces the chances of stockouts and overstocking and improves overall efficiency. For example, a WMS can generate picking lists and guide workers through the most efficient routes, reducing the time spent searching for items.

Automation and technology are transforming warehouse management. Automated systems, such as conveyor belts and robotic pickers, can handle repetitive tasks quickly and accurately, freeing up workers for more complex tasks. Technology like barcode scanners and RFID tags allows for real-time inventory tracking, reducing errors and improving accuracy. Implementing these technologies can lead to significant time and cost savings and increased productivity.

In summary, effective warehouse management involves optimizing the layout and design of the warehouse, following best practices for receiving, storing, and picking inventory, and leveraging technology and automation. By focusing on these areas, we can ensure that our warehouse operates smoothly and efficiently, ultimately leading to better customer service and increased profitability.

INVENTORY AUDITING AND RECONCILIATION

Regular inventory audits are crucial for maintaining the accuracy and integrity of our inventory management system. Conducting these audits helps ensure that the actual physical inventory matches the records in our system. This accuracy is vital for making informed business decisions, fulfilling customer orders, and maintaining financial integrity.

There are several methods for conducting inventory audits. Cycle counting is one effective method, where we count a small portion of the inventory on a regular basis, such as daily or weekly, rather than counting the entire inventory at once. This method is less disruptive to our operations and allows us to identify and correct discrepancies more frequently. On the other hand, physical counts involve a complete count of all inventory items at one time. While more time-consuming, physical counts provide a comprehensive check and are often conducted annually or biannually.

Reconciling discrepancies between physical inventory and records is a critical step in the auditing process. Discrepancies can arise from various sources, such as data entry errors, theft, damage, or misplacement of items. When we find discrepancies, it's important to investigate the cause and make the necessary adjustments to our records. This might involve recounting items, reviewing transaction histories, or implementing stricter controls to prevent future discrepancies.

By conducting regular inventory audits and reconciling any discrepancies, we maintain the accuracy of our inventory records, which in turn helps us manage our stock levels more effectively. Accurate records ensure that we can meet customer demand without overstocking, reduce costs associated with holding excess inventory, and improve overall operational efficiency. Regular audits also help us identify potential issues early, allowing us to address them before they become major problems.

Inventory auditing and reconciliation are essential practices for maintaining accurate and reliable inventory records. Regularly auditing our inventory and addressing any discrepancies ensures that our inventory management system supports our business goals and contributes to our overall success. This diligent approach to inventory management helps us stay on top of our stock, improve efficiency, and maintain high customer satisfaction.

INVENTORY OPTIMIZATION

Inventory optimization is about striking the right balance between having enough stock to meet customer demand and minimizing the costs associated with holding inventory. It's a critical aspect of inventory management that ensures we can fulfill orders promptly without tying up too much capital in unsold goods. Effective inventory optimization helps us avoid the pitfalls of both overstocking and stockouts, which can have significant financial impacts and affect customer satisfaction.

One key technique for optimizing inventory levels is closely monitoring sales trends and adjusting stock levels accordingly. By analyzing historical sales data, we can identify patterns and predict future demand more accurately. This allows us to adjust our inventory levels in anticipation of peak periods or slow seasons. For instance, if we notice a spike in sales for a particular product during the holiday season, we can increase our stock leading up to that period to ensure we meet customer demand.

Another technique is to implement just-in-time (JIT) inventory practices, where we keep inventory levels as low as possible and reorder stock only when needed. This approach reduces holding costs and minimizes the risk of excess inventory becoming obsolete. However, JIT requires a highly reliable supply chain to ensure that we can replenish stock quickly when needed. Establishing strong relationships with suppliers and having contingency plans are essential for this approach's success.

Safety stock is also an important factor in inventory optimization. Keeping a buffer of extra inventory helps us manage unexpected spikes in demand or delays from suppliers. The challenge is to determine the right amount of safety stock to hold without overstocking. This involves calculating the variability in demand and lead time and setting safety stock levels that provide a cushion while minimizing excess.

Inventory optimization software plays a crucial role in streamlining these processes. These tools use advanced algorithms and real-time data to forecast demand, manage stock levels, and automate reordering processes. By integrating with our existing systems, such as our ERP and CRM, inventory optimization software provides a comprehensive view of our inventory and helps us make informed decisions. For example, the software can alert us when stock levels fall below a certain threshold, prompting us to reorder before we run out. It can also analyze sales trends and recommend adjustments to our inventory levels based on predicted demand.

In summary, inventory optimization is about maintaining the right balance of stock to meet customer demand while minimizing costs. We can optimize our inventory levels by using techniques such as sales trend analysis, just-in-time inventory, and safety stock management. Leveraging inventory optimization software enhances these efforts, providing real-time insights and automation that streamline our processes. This balanced approach helps us improve operational efficiency, reduce costs, and ensure customer satisfaction.

FUTURE TRENDS IN INVENTORY MANAGEMENT

The future of inventory management is being shaped by emerging technologies that promise to transform the way we handle stock and streamline our operations. These advancements are set to make inventory management more efficient, accurate, and responsive to market demands.

Emerging technologies like the Internet of Things (IoT) are making it possible to track inventory in real-time with unprecedented precision. Sensors and smart tags on products can provide detailed information about stock levels, location, and condition. This level of visibility helps us make better decisions about when to reorder items and how to optimize storage. For instance, knowing the exact temperature and humidity conditions of a warehouse in real-time can be crucial for products that are sensitive to environmental changes.

Automation and artificial intelligence (AI) are also playing significant roles in the evolution of inventory management. Automated systems can handle repetitive tasks such as restocking shelves, picking and packing orders, and even conducting inventory counts. This speeds up operations and reduces the risk of human error. Conversely, AI can analyze vast amounts of data to predict trends and optimize inventory levels. By leveraging machine learning algorithms, AI can forecast demand more accurately, helping us maintain optimal stock levels and reduce waste.

In a globalized economy, inventory management is becoming increasingly complex. Businesses must navigate supply chains that span multiple countries and continents, dealing with different regulations, cultural norms, and logistical challenges. Technology is helping to bridge these gaps. Advanced software solutions can integrate with various systems across the supply chain, providing a unified view of inventory from production to delivery. This integration helps coordinate efforts across different regions, ensuring that products move smoothly through the supply chain and reach customers on time.

The future of inventory management will likely see more collaborative approaches, with businesses working closely with suppliers and customers to fine-tune inventory practices. Shared data and transparent communication can lead to more synchronized supply chains, where everyone involved can access the same information and make decisions accordingly. This collaboration can help reduce lead times, minimize disruptions, and improve overall efficiency.

The future of inventory management is being shaped by emerging technologies, automation, and AI, all of which are making processes more efficient and accurate. As the global economy continues to evolve, these advancements will help businesses manage their inventory more effectively, navigate complex supply chains, and meet customer demands with greater precision. Embracing these trends will be key to staying competitive and thriving in an increasingly interconnected world.

Conclusion

In this chapter, we've explored the critical components of effective inventory management. We began by defining the purpose of inventory management and its role in ensuring that our business runs smoothly. We looked at various types of inventory, from raw materials to finished goods, and discussed how to manage each type effectively. We also covered essential inventory management techniques like Just-in-Time, Economic Order Quantity, and ABC Analysis, highlighting how these methods help maintain the right balance of stock.

We then delved into inventory control systems, comparing manual and automated methods and examining the benefits of technologies like barcode systems and inventory management software. Demand forecasting was another crucial topic, where we learned how to predict customer demand accurately to avoid overstocking and stockouts. Regular inventory audits and reconciliation were also emphasized to maintain accurate inventory records and ensure operational efficiency.

We wrapped up by discussing inventory optimization, focusing on how to balance inventory levels to meet demand while minimizing costs. Finally, we explored future trends in inventory management, highlighting the impact of emerging technologies, automation, and AI and their role in a globalized economy.

Effective inventory management is not just about keeping track of what's in the warehouse. It's about creating a system that supports our entire business operation, from sourcing and production to sales and customer service. By managing our inventory well, we can reduce costs, improve efficiency, and enhance customer satisfaction. It's a continuous process of monitoring, adjusting, and improving to meet the market's ever-changing demands.

I encourage you to implement the strategies and techniques discussed in this chapter and to continually seek ways to refine and enhance your inventory management practices. By staying proactive and embracing new technologies and methods, we can ensure that our inventory management system remains robust, efficient, and capable of supporting our business goals now and in the future. Effective inventory management is a cornerstone of business success, and investing time and resources into getting it right will pay off in the long run.

4

WAREHOUSING, LOGISTICS, AND FULFILLMENT SOLUTIONS

Warehousing, logistics, and fulfillment are the backbone of any business that deals with physical goods. Their importance cannot be overstated. Efficient warehousing ensures that our inventory is organized, making it easy to locate and manage products. Effective logistics planning guarantees that these products are transported and delivered to customers on time. Fulfillment processes ensure that orders are accurately picked, packed, and shipped. These components create a seamless operation that directly impacts our supply chain efficiency and customer satisfaction.

When warehousing is well-managed, it reduces the time it takes to get products to our customers, minimizes the risk of errors, and keeps costs under control. A well-organized warehouse means that our team can quickly find and process items, which speeds up order fulfillment. This efficiency helps us meet customer expectations for quick and reliable delivery, which is crucial in today's fast-paced market.

Logistics and shipping play a vital role in maintaining this efficiency. Coordinating transportation, managing shipping schedules, and handling returns all require careful planning and execution. When streamlined logistics are streamlined, products move smoothly from our warehouse to the customer's doorstep. This reduces delivery times, lowers shipping costs, and minimizes the risk of damaged goods.

Fulfillment processes are where everything comes together. Accurate picking, packing, and shipping of orders are essential for meeting customer expectations. Errors in fulfillment can lead to returns, additional costs, and, worst of all, dissatisfied customers. By implementing efficient fulfillment practices, we can ensure that each order is handled correctly and delivered on time, maintaining high levels of customer satisfaction.

This chapter will explore several key areas that contribute to effective warehousing, logistics, and fulfillment. We will look at how to design an efficient warehouse layout, best practices for receiving, storing, and picking inventory, and the role of technology in modern warehousing. We'll delve into logistics planning, from selecting transportation modes to managing shipping schedules, and discuss strategies for overcoming common fulfillment challenges.

Additionally, we will cover workforce management, cost management, and sustainability practices within warehousing and logistics. Real-world case studies will provide practical insights, and we'll also examine future trends in the industry, such as automation and AI. By understanding and implementing the strategies discussed in this chapter, we can optimize our operations, reduce costs, and enhance customer satisfaction, ultimately driving our business success.

WAREHOUSE LAYOUT AND DESIGN

Our warehouse's layout and design are critical to our operations' efficiency. A well-thought-out warehouse layout ensures that goods flow smoothly from receiving to storage to shipping. By optimizing this flow, we can reduce the time it takes to process orders and minimize the risk of errors.

The principles of efficient warehouse layout start with understanding the flow of goods. Products should move in a logical sequence from the moment they arrive until they are shipped out. This often means placing receiving areas close to the entrance, storage areas in the middle, and shipping areas near the exit. This setup reduces the distance goods need to travel and streamlines the entire process.

Designing for the optimal flow of goods involves more than just placing areas in a logical sequence. We also need to think about the specific needs of our operations. For example, high-turnover items should be stored closer to the shipping area to reduce picking time. Items that are frequently sold together should be stored near each other to make picking more efficient. This kind of strategic placement can significantly speed up order fulfillment.

Space utilization is another crucial aspect of warehouse design. We need to maximize our storage capacity without compromising accessibility. This often involves effectively using vertical space by installing tall shelving units and ensuring aisles are wide enough for equipment like forklifts. However, we also need to ensure that items are easy to find and access. Efficient use of space means balancing storage density with the need for quick and easy access to items.

Different types of warehouses have different design considerations. For instance, a distribution center that handles a high volume of goods needs a layout that supports rapid processing and movement of large quantities. Storage warehouses, which hold inventory for longer periods, might prioritize maximizing storage space over quick access. Fulfillment centers, which focus on picking and shipping individual orders, need layouts that support efficient picking and packing processes. Each type of warehouse has unique requirements, and our design should reflect the specific needs of our operations.

In summary, designing an efficient warehouse layout involves planning for the optimal flow of goods, maximizing space utilization, and considering the specific needs of different types of warehouses. By focusing on these principles, we can create a warehouse environment that supports our operations, reduces processing times, and enhances overall efficiency. This foundation is crucial for maintaining a smooth and effective supply chain.

WAREHOUSE OPERATIONS

Effective warehouse operations are the backbone of our supply chain, ensuring that goods move smoothly from arrival to delivery. When we receive goods, the process begins with unloading shipments. It's crucial to have a streamlined method for this, as efficient unloading minimizes delays and keeps our operations running smoothly. We need to inspect incoming shipments thoroughly, checking for any damages or discrepancies against the purchase orders. This initial inspection helps prevent issues later in the process and ensures we maintain high quality and accuracy.

Once goods are unloaded and inspected, the next step is storing the inventory. Proper categorization and labeling are essential for easy access and efficient retrieval. By organizing products logically, such as grouping similar items together or arranging them based on their turnover rates, we can optimize our storage space and improve retrieval times. Clear labeling and an organized layout also reduce errors and make it easier for our team to locate items quickly.

When it comes to picking and packing, efficiency is key. The goal is to fulfill orders accurately and swiftly. We use zone picking, where the warehouse is divided into zones, and each worker is responsible for picking items within their zone. This minimizes movement and speeds up the picking process.

Another effective method is batch picking, where we pick multiple orders simultaneously. This reduces the number of trips made through the warehouse and increases productivity. Once picked, items are packed securely to prevent damage during transit. Using standardized packing materials and methods ensures consistency and protects the products.

Shipping is the final step in the warehouse operations process. Preparing and dispatching orders involves several strategies to ensure timely and accurate delivery. We start by verifying that all items are correctly picked and packed. Then, we print shipping labels and organize the orders based on their delivery routes. Grouping shipments by destination helps streamline the loading process and ensures that deliveries are made efficiently. Communication with carriers is crucial to confirm pickup times and manage any potential delays.

We can maintain a smooth and efficient warehouse operation by focusing on best practices for receiving, storing, picking, packing, and shipping. This helps us meet customer expectations for timely deliveries, reduces operational costs, and improves overall productivity. Each step in the process is interconnected, and attention to detail at every stage ensures that we maintain the high standards necessary for success.

STORAGE SOLUTIONS

When it comes to storage solutions, the type of system we choose can significantly impact the efficiency of our warehouse operations. Various storage systems are available, each suited to different kinds of inventory and operational needs. Shelving and racking are the most common, ideal for smaller items, and provide easy access for manual picking. Pallet storage is perfect for handling larger, bulkier items that require forklifts or pallet jacks. For even more efficiency, automated storage and retrieval systems (AS/RS) offer high-tech solutions that can streamline picking and storage processes through robotics and computerized systems.

Choosing the right storage system for our business requires us to assess our specific needs. If we deal with a wide variety of small items, shelving might be the best choice. On the other hand, if our inventory consists mainly of large, heavy goods, pallet storage or racking systems would be more appropriate. Automated systems like AS/RS are a significant investment but can drastically reduce labor costs and improve accuracy and speed in a high-volume warehouse.

Flexibility in our storage solutions is also crucial. Our inventory levels can fluctuate due to seasonality, market trends, or changes in customer demand. Implementing storage systems that can adapt to these changes helps us maintain efficiency. For example, modular shelving units can be easily reconfigured to accommodate different sizes and quantities of inventory. This adaptability ensures that we can respond quickly to changes without significant disruptions to our operations.

Safety is another vital consideration when it comes to storage systems. Ensuring that our storage solutions are safe involves regular maintenance and adherence to industry standards. Shelving and racking systems need to be properly installed and regularly inspected to prevent accidents. Pallet storage requires careful handling to avoid overloading and ensuring that pallets are in good condition. Automated systems need to be equipped with safety features to protect workers from machinery and robotic operations. By prioritizing safety, we create a secure work environment, reduce the risk of accidents, and ensure compliance with regulations.

In summary, selecting the appropriate storage solutions involves evaluating the types of storage systems available, aligning them with our business needs, and ensuring they can adapt to changing inventory levels. Additionally, maintaining a strong focus on safety ensures a secure and efficient warehouse environment. We can optimize our storage capabilities and enhance overall warehouse operations by carefully considering these factors.

TECHNOLOGY IN WAREHOUSING

Technology plays a pivotal role in modern warehousing, transforming the way we manage and track inventory. A Warehouse Management System (WMS) is at the heart of this transformation. A WMS provides real-time visibility into our inventory, helping us manage stock levels, streamline processes, and improve accuracy. It allows us to track every item in the warehouse from the moment it arrives until it is shipped out, ensuring nothing gets lost or misplaced.

Integrating our WMS with other business systems, such as ERP (Enterprise Resource Planning) and CRM (Customer Relationship Management), offers even more benefits. By linking these systems, we create a seamless flow of information across our operations. For example, when a customer places an order through our CRM, the WMS can automatically update inventory levels and generate picking lists. This integration ensures that all departments are working with the same data, reducing errors and improving overall efficiency. It also helps us make more informed decisions by providing a comprehensive view of our business operations.

Barcode and RFID technology further enhance our ability to track inventory accurately. Barcodes are a tried-and-true method for identifying and managing inventory. With a quick scan, we can update our records instantly, reducing the risk of human error. RFID (Radio Frequency Identification) takes this a step further by allowing us to track items without direct line-of-sight. RFID tags can be read automatically as items move through the warehouse, providing real-time updates on their location. This technology is particularly useful for high-volume operations where speed and accuracy are critical. Automation in warehousing is another game-changer. Conveyors, robotic pickers, and automated guided vehicles (AGVs) can handle repetitive tasks faster and more precisely than human workers. Conveyors can transport goods throughout the warehouse quickly and efficiently, reducing the time spent moving items manually. Robotic pickers can retrieve items from shelves and bring them to packing stations, improving picking accuracy and speed. AGVs can navigate the warehouse autonomously, transporting goods to different areas without the need for human intervention. These automated systems free up our employees to focus on more complex tasks, increasing overall productivity.

Incorporating these technologies into our warehouse operations improves efficiency, enhances accuracy, and reduces costs. A WMS integrated with ERP and CRM systems provides a unified platform for managing our operations. Barcode and RFID technology ensure accurate inventory tracking, while automation boosts productivity and reduces labor costs. By embracing these technological advancements, we can maintain a competitive edge in the market and provide better service to our customers. This approach allows us to run a more efficient, reliable, and scalable warehousing operation.

Logistics and Shipping

Logistics and shipping are the lifeblood of our business operations, ensuring that our products reach customers promptly and in perfect condition. Effective logistics planning and coordination are essential to this process. This involves mapping out every step of the journey, from the moment a product leaves our warehouse to the moment it arrives at the customer's door. It's about making sure everything runs smoothly and efficiently, minimizing delays and reducing costs.

Choosing the right transportation modes is a key part of our logistics strategy. Depending on the specifics of the shipment—whether it's time-sensitive, high-value, or a bulk order—we decide between ground, air, or sea transportation. Ground transport is great for domestic deliveries, balancing cost and speed. Air transport, though more expensive, is perfect for urgent deliveries, ensuring products arrive quickly. Sea transport, while slower, is cost-effective for large shipments traveling long distances. By selecting the best transportation method for each scenario, we optimize our logistics for both cost and efficiency.

Managing shipping schedules and deadlines is another crucial aspect. It's not enough to just pick the right transportation mode; we need to ensure that everything runs on time. This involves coordinating with carriers, planning efficient routes, and constantly monitoring the progress of each shipment. We must account for potential delays and have contingency plans ready to address any issues that arise. Keeping everything on schedule is vital for maintaining customer trust and satisfaction.

Handling returns and reverse logistics is also a significant part of our logistics operations. When customers return products, we need a streamlined process to handle these returns efficiently. This includes receiving, inspecting, and restocking returned items or disposing of them if necessary. Effective reverse logistics enhances customer satisfaction and helps us recover costs and manage inventory more effectively.

Real-time shipment tracking and customer communication are essential for building trust and ensuring transparency. Customers want to know where their orders are and when they will arrive. By providing real-time tracking information, we keep them informed at every stage of the shipping process.

This transparency reduces the number of inquiries about order status and builds trust in our reliability. Additionally, proactive communication about any delays or issues helps manage customer expectations and demonstrates our commitment to excellent service.

Effective logistics and shipping require meticulous planning, choosing the right transportation methods, managing schedules, handling returns efficiently, and maintaining clear communication with customers. By focusing on these areas, we can ensure that our products reach customers quickly and reliably, enhancing their overall experience and strengthening our business's reputation. These efforts are crucial for maintaining a smooth supply chain and achieving long-term success.

INVENTORY MANAGEMENT WITHIN THE WAREHOUSE

Effective inventory management within the warehouse is essential for keeping our operations running smoothly. One of the key aspects of this is maintaining accurate inventory records. This accuracy is the foundation of all our inventory processes, ensuring we always know what we have. We use various techniques to achieve this, such as regular updates to our inventory management system whenever stock is added or removed. Barcode and RFID technology play a crucial role here, allowing us to scan items quickly and accurately, reducing the risk of human error.

Conducting regular inventory audits and reconciliations is another critical practice. These audits help us verify that our physical inventory matches the records in our system. By regularly comparing our stock counts to our inventory data, we can catch discrepancies early and investigate their causes. This might involve counting a subset of items daily, weekly, or monthly—a process known as cycle counting—or performing full physical counts periodically. Reconciling any differences helps maintain the integrity of our inventory records, ensuring that our data remains reliable.

Managing seasonal inventory fluctuations requires strategic planning and flexibility. We need to anticipate periods of high demand, such as holidays or special promotions, and adjust our inventory levels accordingly. This means increasing our stock of popular items in advance and ensuring that we have enough storage space to accommodate these additional goods. Conversely, we might reduce our inventory levels during slower periods to avoid excess stock that could tie up capital and storage space. By closely monitoring sales trends and using demand forecasting tools, we can better predict these fluctuations and plan our inventory accordingly.

Real-time inventory visibility is crucial for making informed decisions and maintaining operational efficiency. When we have up-to-the-minute data on our inventory levels, we can respond quickly to changes in demand, manage stockouts, and reduce excess inventory. Real-time visibility also improves our ability to fulfill orders accurately and promptly, as we always know exactly what is available. This requires integrating our inventory management system with other business systems, such as ERP and CRM, to ensure seamless data flow and instant updates.

In summary, effective inventory management within the warehouse involves maintaining accurate records, conducting regular audits, managing seasonal fluctuations, and ensuring real-time visibility. These practices help us keep our operations running smoothly, reduce costs, and enhance customer satisfaction. By staying on top of our inventory management processes, we can ensure that we always have the right products available at the right time, supporting our overall business success.

OVERCOMING FULFILLMENT CHALLENGES

Overcoming fulfillment challenges is critical to maintaining a smooth and efficient supply chain. In dealing with physical goods, we often encounter common challenges such as delays, errors, and unexpected disruptions. These issues can arise from various sources, including supplier delays, transportation problems, or even internal miscommunications. Addressing these challenges promptly and effectively is essential to keep our operations running smoothly and to ensure customer satisfaction.

Managing delays and errors starts with a robust system for tracking and monitoring all stages of the fulfillment process. By using advanced tracking tools and maintaining clear communication with suppliers and carriers, we can anticipate potential issues and take proactive measures to mitigate them. For instance, having backup suppliers or alternative shipping routes can help us avoid significant delays when our primary options fall through. Additionally, implementing quality control checks at various points in the process helps catch errors early, reducing the impact on the final delivery.

Improving order accuracy and delivery speed requires a combination of technology and streamlined processes. Automated inventory management, picking, and packing systems can significantly reduce the likelihood of errors and speed up the fulfillment process. For example, using barcode scanners or RFID technology ensures that the correct items are picked and packed, while automated sorting systems can handle large volumes of orders quickly and accurately. Training our staff thoroughly and continuously improving our workflow is vital in enhancing order accuracy and delivery speed.

Handling customer complaints and returns efficiently is crucial for maintaining a positive relationship with our customers. When a customer has an issue, it's important to address it promptly and professionally. This involves having a clear and straightforward returns process that customers can follow. By providing prepaid return labels and offering multiple return options, we can make the process as hassle-free as possible for our customers. Additionally, keeping customers informed throughout the returns process, from the moment they initiate a return to the final resolution, helps build trust and loyalty.

In summary, overcoming fulfillment challenges involves managing delays and errors with proactive measures, improving order accuracy and delivery speed through technology and streamlined processes, and efficiently handling customer complaints and returns. By focusing on these areas, we can ensure that our fulfillment operations remain reliable and effective, ultimately enhancing customer satisfaction and supporting the growth of our business. Maintaining a flexible and responsive approach allows us to adapt to any challenges that come our way, keeping our supply chain robust and our customers happy.

Workforce Management

Effective workforce management is crucial for the smooth operation of our warehouse and logistics functions. The first step is hiring the right people. We need individuals who are not only skilled and experienced but also fit well with our company culture. During the hiring process, we look for candidates who show reliability, attention to detail, and the ability to work well under pressure. Once we have the right people on board, training becomes the next priority. Comprehensive training programs ensure that our staff understands their roles, the processes they need to follow, and how to use any equipment or technology we have in place. This training not only improves efficiency but also helps reduce errors and accidents.

Implementing efficient labor management practices is another key aspect. This involves scheduling shifts effectively to ensure we have enough staff during peak times without overstaffing during slower periods. Using labor management software can help us track performance, manage time-off requests, and optimize scheduling. This software provides real-time data that allows us to make informed decisions about staffing levels and adjust as needed to meet demand.

Ensuring workplace safety and compliance with regulations is non-negotiable. A safe working environment protects our employees and minimizes disruptions caused by accidents. We adhere to all relevant health and safety regulations, regularly conduct safety drills, and keep our equipment well-maintained. Safety training is a continuous process, not a one-time event. We keep our staff updated on best practices and ensure that everyone understands the importance of following safety protocols. Compliance with these standards keeps our operations running smoothly and builds a culture of safety and accountability.

Motivating and retaining employees is essential for maintaining a stable and productive workforce. Competitive wages and benefits are a start, but we also focus on creating a positive work environment where employees feel valued and engaged. Regular feedback, opportunities for career advancement, and recognizing hard work all contribute to employee satisfaction. By investing in our people, we foster loyalty and reduce turnover, saving recruitment costs and preserving institutional knowledge within the company.

Effective workforce management involves careful hiring and training, efficient labor management, a strong focus on safety and compliance, and strategies to motivate and retain employees. We create a productive, engaged, and stable workforce that supports our overall business goals by focusing on these areas. This approach not only enhances operational efficiency but also builds a strong, cohesive team dedicated to the success of our company.

COST MANAGEMENT IN WAREHOUSING AND LOGISTICS

Managing costs in warehousing and logistics is crucial for maintaining a healthy bottom line. Identifying and reducing costs starts with a detailed analysis of our current expenses. We look at everything from labor and equipment to utilities and materials. By breaking down these costs, we can pinpoint areas where we might be overspending or where efficiencies can be introduced. For example, if we notice that labor costs are particularly high during certain times of the day, we might adjust our scheduling to better match our workforce with our workload.

Optimizing energy usage and reducing utility costs are other important aspects of cost management. Warehouses often consume significant energy, so finding ways to cut back can lead to substantial savings. We employ some strategies to install energy-efficient lighting, optimize heating and cooling systems, and use programmable thermostats. Additionally, conducting regular energy audits helps us identify and address areas where energy might be wasted. Implementing these changes not only reduces costs but also supports our sustainability goals.

Managing maintenance and repair costs for equipment is equally important. Regular maintenance helps prevent breakdowns and extends the lifespan of our equipment, reducing the need for costly repairs or replacements. We have a schedule for routine inspections and maintenance tasks to ensure that everything runs smoothly. When repairs are necessary, we try to handle them promptly to avoid prolonged downtime. Investing in high-quality equipment initially can also save money in the long run, as it tends to be more durable and reliable.

Working with third-party logistics providers (3PLs) can also offer cost-saving opportunities. These providers often have the expertise and resources to handle logistics more efficiently than we could manage in-house. However, it's essential to evaluate and negotiate with them carefully. We assess their performance, reliability, and the cost of their services. Negotiating favorable terms and building strong relationships with our 3PLs can improve rates and service levels. Regularly reviewing these partnerships ensures that we're getting the best value for our investment.

Cost management in warehousing and logistics involves a multifaceted approach. We can significantly lower our operating costs by identifying and reducing unnecessary expenses, optimizing energy usage, managing maintenance costs, and negotiating effectively with 3PLs. These efforts help us maintain a lean, efficient operation supporting our business's profitability and sustainability.

SUSTAINABILITY IN WAREHOUSING AND LOGISTICS

Sustainability in warehousing and logistics is more than just a trend; it's a necessary evolution for modern businesses. Implementing eco-friendly practices in our warehouse operations begins with a commitment to reducing our environmental footprint. We start by evaluating every aspect of our operations to identify areas where we can make a positive impact. This includes rethinking how we use resources, manage waste, and consume energy.

Reducing waste and promoting recycling are critical components of our sustainability efforts. We focus on minimizing waste at the source by adopting practices like reusing packaging materials and optimizing inventory to avoid overstock and spoilage. In addition, we set up comprehensive recycling programs for materials such as cardboard, plastic, and metal. By creating a culture of recycling, we encourage our employees to participate actively in these initiatives, making sustainability a part of our everyday operations.

Energy-efficient lighting, heating, and cooling systems play a significant role in reducing our energy consumption. We have upgraded our warehouse lighting to LED bulbs, which use less energy and have a longer lifespan than traditional incandescent bulbs. Our heating and cooling systems are optimized with programmable thermostats and regular maintenance to ensure they operate efficiently. These changes lower our utility bills and reduce our carbon footprint, contributing to a healthier planet.

The benefits of sustainable practices extend beyond environmental impact. These practices lead to cost savings, improved efficiency, and a stronger brand reputation for our business. Customers and clients increasingly prefer to do business with companies that demonstrate a commitment to sustainability. By showcasing our eco-friendly practices, we attract and retain environmentally conscious customers, which can boost our sales and market share.

Moreover, sustainable practices can enhance employee satisfaction and retention. Our staff takes pride in working for a company that values environmental stewardship. This sense of purpose and alignment with our values fosters a positive work environment and strengthens our team's dedication to our business goals.

Sustainability in warehousing and logistics involves implementing eco-friendly practices, reducing waste, promoting recycling, and optimizing energy use. These efforts benefit the environment and provide significant advantages for our business, including cost savings, improved efficiency, and a stronger market position. Committing to sustainability creates a positive impact that resonates with our customers, employees, and the broader community, paving the way for long-term success.

FUTURE TRENDS IN WAREHOUSING AND LOGISTICS

The future of warehousing and logistics is poised for significant transformation, driven by emerging technologies that promise to reshape our industry. Technologies such as the Internet of Things (IoT), blockchain, and advanced robotics are already starting to make their mark, offering new levels of efficiency, transparency, and automation. The potential impact of these technologies is immense, promising to streamline operations and reduce costs while enhancing accuracy and speed.

Automation, AI, and machine learning are at the forefront of this technological revolution. Automation is not just about replacing manual labor with machines; it's about integrating intelligent systems that can continually learn and adapt to improve performance. For instance, automated guided vehicles (AGVs) and drones are becoming more prevalent in warehouses, handling tasks like inventory counts and order picking with remarkable precision. AI and machine learning algorithms analyze vast amounts of data to predict demand, optimize routes, and manage inventory levels dynamically. These advancements allow us to operate more efficiently, reducing waste and improving our response times to market changes.

In a globalized economy, the future of warehousing and logistics will be characterized by increased connectivity and collaboration across borders. Supply chains are becoming more complex, with components sourced from multiple countries and products shipped worldwide. This complexity necessitates more sophisticated logistics solutions that can handle the nuances of international trade. Advanced software platforms that integrate with global networks will become essential, enabling real-time tracking, customs management, and compliance with international regulations.

Looking ahead, we can predict several key trends that will shape the evolution of warehousing and logistics. First, the adoption of autonomous vehicles and drones for last-mile delivery will become more widespread, driven by the need for faster and more reliable shipping options. Second, we will see greater use of blockchain technology to enhance supply chain transparency and security, providing an immutable record of transactions that can be trusted by all parties involved. Third, environmental sustainability will remain a priority, with more companies adopting green logistics practices to reduce their carbon footprint and appeal to eco-conscious consumers.

The convergence of these trends points to a future where warehousing and logistics are more efficient, transparent, and sustainable. Businesses that embrace these advancements will be better positioned to navigate the challenges of a globalized economy, respond quickly to changes in demand, and meet customers' growing expectations for speed and reliability.

In summary, the future of warehousing and logistics is bright, with emerging technologies, automation, AI, and a globalized approach driving significant changes. By staying ahead of these trends and investing in the right technologies, we can ensure our operations remain competitive and resilient, ready to meet the demands of a rapidly evolving marketplace.

CONCLUSION

In this chapter, we have delved into the essential components of warehousing, logistics, and fulfillment. We discussed the principles of efficient warehouse layout and design, the importance of effective warehouse operations, and the various storage solutions that help optimize space and efficiency. We also explored the critical role of technology in modern warehousing, from Warehouse Management Systems (WMS) to automation and RFID tracking, and how these tools enhance accuracy and productivity.

Additionally, we covered logistics planning and coordination, emphasizing the selection of appropriate transportation modes, managing shipping schedules, and handling returns. We underscored the significance of real-time shipment tracking and transparent communication with customers, which build trust and ensure customer satisfaction. Addressing common fulfillment challenges, we examined strategies for managing delays, improving order accuracy, and efficiently handling customer complaints and returns.

Effective warehousing, logistics, and fulfillment are the backbone of any successful supply chain. They ensure that products move smoothly from storage to the customer's hands, minimizing delays and errors while maximizing efficiency and customer satisfaction. These elements are not just about keeping the warehouse organized or getting shipments out on time—they are about creating a seamless operation that supports the entire business. Investing in these areas can reduce costs, enhance service levels, and build a stronger, more resilient operation.

Continuous evaluation and improvement are vital in maintaining high standards. The landscape of warehousing and logistics is constantly evolving with new technologies and changing market demands. We can stay ahead of the curve by regularly reviewing our processes, embracing new technologies, and being open to change. It's important to foster a culture of continuous improvement, where feedback is valued and innovation is encouraged. This proactive approach ensures that we can adapt to any challenges and seize new opportunities as they arise.

The effectiveness of our warehousing, logistics, and fulfillment operations directly impacts our business success. By focusing on these key areas and committing to continuous improvement, we can create a robust supply chain that not only meets but exceeds customer expectations. This dedication to excellence will help us thrive in a competitive market and drive long-term growth and profitability.

5

FULFILLMENT
OF DIGITAL GOODS

The fulfillment of digital goods has become increasingly important in today's market. With the rapid advancement of technology and the growing preference for instant access to products, the demand for digital goods is higher than ever. Digital goods include items such as software, e-books, online courses, and digital media. Unlike physical goods, these products can be delivered instantly to customers anywhere in the world, offering a significant advantage in terms of convenience and speed.

One of the key differences between physical and digital goods fulfillment is the nature of the delivery process. Physical goods require warehousing, shipping, and handling, which involve logistical challenges and costs. In contrast, digital goods can be delivered electronically, eliminating the need for physical storage and transportation. This not only reduces overhead costs but also allows for instantaneous delivery, enhancing customer satisfaction.

Another notable difference is inventory management. With physical goods, we must carefully manage stock levels to avoid overstocking or running out of products. Digital goods, however, do not have such constraints. Once a digital product is created, it can be duplicated and distributed indefinitely without the risk of stockouts or excess inventory. This makes inventory management for digital goods much simpler and more cost-effective.

In this chapter, we will explore several key areas related to the fulfillment of digital goods. We will start by defining what digital goods are and providing examples to illustrate the variety of products that fall into this category. We will then discuss the benefits of selling digital goods, including instant delivery, low overhead costs, and global reach.

Understanding digital goods is essential for grasping their potential in the market. Digital goods encompass a wide range of products, from software that powers our devices to e-books that provide knowledge and entertainment. Online courses offer educational opportunities, while digital media, such as music and movies, deliver entertainment instantly. These products share common characteristics: they are intangible, can be delivered electronically, and often come with intellectual property protections.

Selling digital goods offers numerous benefits. The ability to deliver products instantly meets the growing consumer demand for immediate gratification. Customers no longer need to wait for shipping; they can access their purchases immediately. This instant delivery improves customer satisfaction and increases the likelihood of repeat purchases.

Low overhead costs are another significant advantage. Without the need for physical storage or shipping, the expenses associated with digital goods are minimal. This allows businesses to allocate resources more efficiently and focus on enhancing product quality and customer service.

Moreover, digital goods have a global reach. Unlike physical products, which geographic boundaries and shipping constraints may limit, digital goods can be delivered to customers anywhere in the world with an internet connection. This opens up vast markets and opportunities for growth, allowing businesses to reach a broader audience and expand their customer base.

The following sections will delve into the infrastructure required for digital goods fulfillment, including the setup of robust digital delivery systems and the importance of security and protection. We will discuss payment processing, order processing, and delivery methods tailored for digital goods. Additionally, we will explore the role of customer support, marketing strategies, and legal considerations unique to digital products. Finally, we will examine analytics and performance tracking to understand how data-driven decisions can enhance digital goods fulfillment.

By the end of this chapter, you will have a comprehensive understanding of the fulfillment of digital goods and practical strategies to optimize this process for your business.

Infrastructure for Digital Goods Fulfillment

Creating a robust infrastructure for digital goods fulfillment is essential for delivering a seamless experience to our customers. Setting up a reliable digital delivery system is the foundation of this process. It involves ensuring that our digital products can be delivered quickly and efficiently to customers worldwide. This means investing in technology that supports high-speed downloads, secure transactions, and easy access.

Choosing the right platform for distributing digital goods is another critical decision. E-commerce platforms like Shopify or WooCommerce are popular choices because they offer comprehensive solutions for selling and managing digital products. These platforms provide the tools we need to handle everything from payment processing to customer service.

Alternatively, digital content delivery networks (CDNs) like Amazon Web Services or Akamai can be used to ensure fast and reliable delivery of digital content. CDNs distribute our products across multiple servers around the world, reducing latency and improving download speeds for customers no matter where they are located.

Ensuring the scalability and reliability of our digital delivery systems is paramount as our business grows. We need systems that can handle increasing amounts of traffic without compromising performance. This means investing in infrastructure that can scale up quickly to meet demand during peak times, such as during a major product launch or a holiday sale. It also means having redundancy built into our systems to prevent downtime. If one server fails, another can take over seamlessly, ensuring that our customers can always access their purchases.

Reliability also extends to security. We must protect our digital goods from unauthorized access and piracy. Implementing digital rights management (DRM) and encryption can help safeguard our content, ensuring that only paying customers can access it. This protects our revenue and builds trust with our customers, who can feel confident that their purchases are secure.

Security, Protection, and Payment Processing

Security and protection are critical aspects of managing digital goods. Securing our products against piracy and unauthorized access is essential to protecting our revenue and maintaining the trust of our customers. Digital goods are especially vulnerable to piracy because they can be easily copied and distributed. To combat this, we must implement robust security measures.

Digital rights management (DRM) and encryption are two key tools in our security arsenal. DRM helps control our digital products' use, preventing unauthorized copying and sharing. Encryption ensures that data is protected during transmission and storage, making it difficult for hackers to access our content. These measures work together to safeguard our products and give our customers confidence that their purchases are secure.

Protecting customer data and maintaining privacy is just as important as securing our digital goods. We collect sensitive information from our customers, such as payment details and personal data, which must be kept secure. Implementing best practices for data protection, such as using secure servers and encrypting sensitive information, helps prevent data breaches. Additionally, we must ensure compliance with privacy laws and regulations, such as the General Data Protection Regulation (GDPR), to protect our customers' rights and maintain their trust.

Payment processing is another critical component of digital goods fulfillment. Integrating secure and efficient payment gateways is essential for providing a smooth and trustworthy purchasing experience. Customers need to feel confident that their payment information is safe when they make a purchase. We work with reliable payment processors like PayPal, Stripe, and others that offer robust security features and fraud protection. This helps minimize the risk of payment fraud and ensures that transactions are processed quickly and securely.

Handling various payment methods is also important for meeting the needs of our diverse customer base. Multiple payment options, such as credit cards, PayPal, and even cryptocurrencies, make it easier for customers to complete their purchases. This flexibility can increase conversion rates and improve customer satisfaction.

Managing refunds and chargebacks is a necessary part of running an online business. This can be particularly challenging for digital goods due to the nature of the products. Clear refund policies and prompt customer service are essential for handling these situations effectively. By providing a straightforward refund process and promptly addressing customer concerns, we can maintain customer trust and minimize disputes. Chargebacks, where a customer disputes a transaction and requests a reversal from their bank, require careful management to protect our business from fraud and loss. Implementing measures to verify transactions and respond to chargeback requests quickly can help reduce the impact on our bottom line.

Order Processing and Delivery

Order processing and delivery for digital goods require a streamlined and efficient system to ensure customers receive their purchases instantly and without hassle. Automated order processing workflows are the backbone of this system. By automating the process, we can handle orders quickly and accurately, reducing the risk of errors and delays. When a customer places an order, the system automatically verifies payment, processes the order, and triggers the delivery mechanism. This speeds up the process and frees up time for our team to focus on other important tasks.

Instant delivery mechanisms are a key feature of digital goods fulfillment. Customers expect to receive their digital products immediately after purchase, whether it's software, an e-book, or an online course. We use various delivery methods to meet this expectation. Email delivery is common, where customers receive a link to download their product directly in their inbox. Direct downloads from our website are another popular option, allowing customers to access their purchases immediately after checkout. For some products, such as software or online services, we provide access codes for customers to unlock their purchases.

Managing download limits and expiration for digital products is essential to protect our content and ensure fair use. Setting download limits helps prevent unauthorized sharing and excessive downloads. For example, we might allow a customer to download a purchased e-book up to five times. This is usually sufficient for personal use while discouraging distribution to others. Expiration dates can also be applied to certain digital products, such as access to an online course. By setting a timeframe in which the product can be accessed, we create a sense of urgency and encourage customers to use the product within a reasonable period.

These practices help us maintain control over our digital goods while providing our customers with a smooth and satisfying experience. Automation ensures that orders are processed quickly and accurately, meeting the high expectations of digital consumers. Instant delivery mechanisms provide immediate gratification, which is a significant advantage of digital products over physical ones. By managing download limits and expiration dates, we protect our intellectual property and ensure that our customers use their purchases appropriately.

Effective order processing and delivery are crucial for the success of our digital goods. Automation, instant delivery, and careful management of download limits and expiration dates ensure that our customers receive their purchases quickly and efficiently while protecting our content. These strategies help us maintain a high level of customer satisfaction and support the growth and sustainability of our business.

Customer Support for Digital Goods

Customer support for digital goods is crucial to maintaining a high level of customer satisfaction and ensuring that our customers have a seamless experience with our products. Providing effective customer support means being accessible, responsive, and knowledgeable. It's essential to offer multiple channels through which customers can reach us, such as email, live chat, and phone support. This ensures that no matter what issue arises, our customers can get the help they need quickly and efficiently.

Common issues with digital goods often revolve around download problems and access issues. Customers might have trouble downloading their purchases due to browser settings, network issues, or incompatible devices. Addressing these problems requires a combination of clear communication and technical expertise. For instance, we need to guide customers through troubleshooting steps, such as clearing their browser cache, checking their internet connection, or trying a different device. In cases involving access codes, ensuring that customers know how to use them correctly is vital. Clear instructions on redeeming codes and troubleshooting common errors can prevent many access issues.

To assist customers effectively, we use a combination of FAQs, tutorials, and support tickets. FAQs are a valuable resource for addressing common questions and problems. By providing detailed answers to frequently asked questions, we can help customers resolve many issues on their own, reducing the need for direct support. Tutorials in written, video, or interactive formats offer step-by-step guidance on using our digital products. These tutorials can cover everything from downloading and installing software to accessing online courses. They empower customers to navigate their issues independently, enhancing their overall experience with our products.

When customers require more personalized assistance, support tickets come into play. Our support ticket system allows customers to submit detailed descriptions of their problems, which we can then address individually. This system ensures that our support team handles more complex issues with the attention and care they deserve. Prompt responses and clear, helpful solutions are key to resolving these issues satisfactorily.

Providing effective customer support for digital goods involves being accessible, addressing common issues efficiently, and offering a variety of support resources. By using FAQs, tutorials, and support tickets, we can assist our customers in navigating and resolving their problems, ensuring a positive experience with our digital products. This approach not only enhances customer satisfaction but also builds trust and loyalty, supporting the long-term success of our business.

Marketing and Promotion of Digital Goods

Marketing and promoting digital goods require a strategic approach to stand out in a crowded marketplace. One effective strategy is content marketing. We can attract and engage our target audience by creating valuable and relevant content. This might involve writing blog posts, producing videos, or hosting webinars showcasing our digital products' benefits and features. Providing educational content that addresses our customers' pain points can position us as experts in our field, building trust and encouraging sales.

Social media is another powerful tool for promoting digital goods. Platforms like Facebook, Instagram, and Twitter allow us to reach a broad audience and engage with potential customers in real-time. Sharing updates, promotions, and customer testimonials can generate buzz around our products and foster a community of loyal followers. Social media advertising also enables us to target specific demographics, ensuring our promotions reach the most relevant audience.

Email campaigns are essential for maintaining direct communication with our customers. By building an email list of interested prospects and existing customers, we can send personalized messages that promote new products, offer exclusive discounts, and provide valuable information. Regular newsletters keep our audience engaged and informed about our latest offerings, encouraging repeat purchases and fostering customer loyalty.

Leveraging online platforms and marketplaces can significantly expand our reach. Selling our digital products on established platforms like Amazon, Etsy, or specialized digital marketplaces exposes us to a vast audience that we might not reach through our channels alone. These platforms often have built-in marketing tools and a ready-made customer base, making it easier to gain visibility and credibility.

Offering discounts, bundles, and loyalty programs attract and retain customers. Discounts and special promotions create a sense of urgency and encourage immediate purchases. Bundling products at a reduced price can add value to customers while increasing our average order value. Loyalty programs reward repeat customers with exclusive benefits, such as discounts on future purchases or early access to new products. These programs incentivize continued engagement and make customers feel valued and appreciated.

Marketing and promoting digital goods involve a multifaceted approach, including content marketing, social media, email campaigns, leveraging online platforms, and offering incentives like discounts and loyalty programs. By employing these strategies, we can effectively reach our target audience, generate interest in our products, and build a loyal customer base. These efforts are essential for driving sales and ensuring the long-term success of our digital goods.

LEGAL CONSIDERATIONS

Navigating the legal landscape for digital goods requires a thorough understanding of copyright and intellectual property laws. These laws protect our creations, ensuring that we retain the rights to our digital products and prevent unauthorized use or distribution. Knowing how to register our copyrights, what protections we have under the law, and how to enforce these rights if someone infringes upon them is crucial. This knowledge safeguards our business and ensures that we can fully capitalize on our intellectual property.

Complying with international regulations for digital sales is another vital aspect. Selling digital goods online means our customer base can be global, and each country may have different rules regarding digital transactions. This includes tax regulations, consumer protection laws, and data privacy requirements. For example, the General Data Protection Regulation (GDPR) in Europe imposes strict rules on how businesses collect, store, and use personal data. We must ensure that our practices are in line with these regulations to avoid hefty fines and legal issues. Staying updated on international laws and adapting our practices accordingly is essential for maintaining a smooth operation and fostering trust with our global customers.

Drafting clear terms of service and privacy policies is fundamental to establishing transparent and trustworthy relationships with our customers. Our terms of service should outline the rules and guidelines for using our digital products, including what customers can and cannot do with the content they purchase. This helps prevent misuse and clarifies our rights and responsibilities as well as those of our customers.

A well-crafted privacy policy is equally important. It should detail how we collect, use, and protect customer information, ensuring that we comply with all relevant data protection laws. This transparency builds trust with our customers and provides legal protection for our business.

In summary, understanding copyright and intellectual property laws, complying with international regulations, and drafting clear terms of service and privacy policies are critical components of managing the legal aspects of digital goods. These measures protect our business, ensure compliance with global standards, and foster trust with our customers, supporting the long-term success of our digital products.

ANALYTICS AND PERFORMANCE TRACKING

Tracking sales and performance metrics for our digital goods is essential for understanding how our products perform and identifying improvement areas. By monitoring these metrics, we can gain valuable insights into our sales trends, customer preferences, and overall business health. This data helps us make informed decisions about product development, marketing strategies, and customer support.

Using analytics tools allows us to dive deeper into customer behavior and product usage. Tools like Google Analytics, for example, provide detailed reports on how customers interact with our website, from the pages they visit to the actions they take. We can see which products are most popular, how long customers spend on our site, and where they drop off in the purchase process. This information is invaluable for optimizing our website and ensuring a smooth user experience. Tools like Mixpanel or Hotjar can also help us understand how customers use our digital goods, offering insights into how we can enhance our products to better meet their needs.

Making data-driven decisions is crucial for improving the fulfillment of our digital goods. We can identify patterns and trends that inform our strategies by analyzing the data we collect. For instance, if we notice that a particular product consistently underperforms, we might investigate further to understand why. Maybe the product description isn't clear, or perhaps there are technical issues that need to be addressed. On the other hand, if a product is performing exceptionally well, we can look for ways to capitalize on that success, such as developing complementary products or enhancing marketing efforts.

Analytics also help us track the effectiveness of our marketing campaigns. We can see which channels drive the most traffic and conversions, allowing us to allocate our marketing budget more effectively. If we find that email campaigns result in higher sales than social media ads, we might decide to focus more resources on building our email list and crafting compelling email content.

Furthermore, performance tracking helps us understand customer satisfaction and loyalty. By monitoring metrics such as repeat purchase rates and customer feedback, we can gauge how well our digital goods meet customer expectations. This information is vital for making improvements and ensuring we continue providing value to our customers.

Tracking sales and performance metrics, using analytics tools to monitor customer behavior, and making data-driven decisions are essential practices for optimizing digital goods fulfillment. These efforts enable us to understand our business better, make informed strategic choices, and continually improve our products and services, ensuring long-term success and customer satisfaction.

JASON MILLER

Future Trends in Digital Goods Fulfillment

The future of digital goods fulfillment is set to be shaped by emerging technologies that promise to revolutionize the way we deliver, secure, and engage with digital products. Technologies such as artificial intelligence (AI), blockchain, and augmented reality (AR) are already making waves and are likely to profoundly impact our industry.

AI, for instance, is enhancing the way we personalize customer experiences. By analyzing vast amounts of data, AI can help us understand customer preferences and behaviors more deeply, allowing us to tailor our offerings and recommendations. This personalization improves customer satisfaction and drives sales by presenting customers with products that are most relevant to their needs.

Blockchain technology offers exciting possibilities for enhancing the security and transparency of digital goods transactions. With blockchain, we can create immutable records of ownership and transfer, making it nearly impossible for unauthorized users to copy or distribute our digital products. This technology also simplifies the process of verifying the authenticity of digital goods, providing customers with greater confidence in their purchases.

Augmented reality is another emerging trend that could transform digital goods fulfillment. AR can offer customers immersive experiences, allowing them to interact with digital products in a more engaging and interactive way. For example, customers could preview how digital art might look on their walls or explore a virtual tour of a digital course before purchasing. This level of interaction can help customers make more informed decisions and enhance their overall experience.

In terms of digital delivery, we are seeing trends toward faster, more reliable methods. Cloud-based solutions are becoming more prevalent, allowing for seamless and instant access to digital goods from anywhere in the world. These platforms offer the scalability needed to handle increasing demand, ensuring that our delivery systems remain robust and efficient as our customer base grows.

Security continues to be a major focus, with advancements in encryption and digital rights management (DRM) providing stronger protections against piracy and unauthorized access. As cyber threats evolve, so too must our security measures. Staying ahead of these threats requires ongoing investment in the latest security technologies and practices.

Customer engagement is also evolving, with an emphasis on creating more interactive and personalized experiences. This could involve leveraging social media platforms, gamification, and other innovative approaches to keep customers engaged and loyal. Building a community around our digital products can foster a sense of belonging and encourage repeat purchases.

Looking ahead, we can expect the fulfillment of digital goods to become even more streamlined and customer-centric. The integration of AI, blockchain, and AR, combined with advances in delivery and security, will create a more efficient and secure ecosystem for digital goods. These technologies will enhance the customer experience and provide us with new tools to manage and protect our digital assets.

In summary, the future of digital goods fulfillment is bright, driven by emerging technologies and evolving trends that promise to enhance delivery, security, and customer engagement. By staying informed and adaptable, we can leverage these advancements to improve our offerings and ensure the continued success of our business in the digital age.

CONCLUSION

In this chapter, we've explored the essential elements of digital goods fulfillment, from setting up robust delivery systems and securing our products to providing excellent customer support and leveraging data analytics. We've discussed how emerging technologies like AI, blockchain, and augmented reality are poised to revolutionize our industry, offering new ways to enhance security, streamline delivery, and engage customers.

Efficient and secure fulfillment of digital goods is not just a matter of operational necessity; it's a cornerstone of our business's success. Ensuring that our digital products are delivered quickly and reliably while protecting them from unauthorized access builds trust with our customers. This trust is essential for fostering long-term relationships and encouraging repeat business.

Moreover, as the landscape of digital goods continues to evolve, so must our strategies and practices. It is crucial to remain adaptable and forward-thinking. By continuously evaluating and improving our digital goods fulfillment processes, we can stay ahead of the curve and meet the ever-changing demands of our customers. This means staying informed about the latest technological advancements, being vigilant about security threats, and always looking for ways to enhance the customer experience.

The fulfillment of digital goods is a dynamic and integral part of our business operations. By focusing on efficiency, security, and customer satisfaction, we can ensure that our digital products meet the highest standards and continue to drive our business forward. Continuous improvement is key—by regularly assessing our practices and embracing new technologies, we can maintain a competitive edge and achieve sustained success in the digital marketplace.

6

CHOOSING AND USING E-COMMERCE PLATFORMS

Selecting the right e-commerce platform is crucial for the success of your online business. This decision influences not just the daily operations of your store but also your ability to scale, adapt, and meet customer expectations. A suitable platform can streamline processes, enhance customer experience, and support your business growth. Conversely, a poor choice can lead to inefficiencies, security vulnerabilities, and missed opportunities.

When choosing an e-commerce platform, several vital considerations come into play. You need a user-friendly interface that makes managing your store straightforward. Customization options are essential for ensuring your store reflects your brand identity. Integration capabilities with payment gateways and other tools are essential for smooth operations. Mobile responsiveness is crucial as more customers shop on their phones. Security features protect your business and customers, while scalability ensures your platform can grow with your business. Finally, reliable customer support and resources can help you navigate any issues.

In this chapter, we'll delve into these considerations in detail. We'll explore what e-commerce platforms are and what their purpose is. We'll compare different types of platforms, including hosted versus self-hosted and open-source versus proprietary options. We'll look at examples of popular platforms like Shopify, WooCommerce, and Magento. We'll also discuss key features to look for in a platform, provide a detailed comparison of top platforms, and weigh the pros and cons of each.

Understanding E-commerce Platforms

E-commerce platforms are software solutions designed to help businesses set up and manage online stores. They provide tools for listing products, processing payments, managing inventory, and fulfilling orders. The primary purpose of an e-commerce platform is to facilitate online transactions between businesses and customers, ensuring a smooth and efficient shopping experience.

There are various types of e-commerce platforms to consider. Hosted platforms, such as Shopify and BigCommerce, manage the technical aspects for you, offering convenience and ease of use. These platforms handle everything from server maintenance to security updates, allowing you to focus on running your business. Self-hosted platforms, like WooCommerce and Magento, provide more control and customization options. However, they require more technical knowledge and resources to manage. Open-source platforms offer the flexibility to modify the code and tailor the platform to your specific needs. In contrast, proprietary platforms have dedicated support and built-in features but may be less flexible.

Popular e-commerce platforms include Shopify, known for its ease of use and comprehensive features; WooCommerce, a flexible and customizable option built on WordPress; and

Magento, a powerful platform ideal for larger businesses with complex needs.

Key Features to Look for in an E-commerce Platform

A user-friendly interface is crucial for efficiently managing your store. The platform should simplify tasks such as adding products, processing orders, and handling customer inquiries. Customization options allow you to create a unique shopping experience that aligns with your brand. Look for platforms that offer flexibility in design and functionality, enabling you to tailor your store to your specific needs.

Integration with payment gateways and other essential tools is vital for smooth operations. Your platform should easily connect with payment processors, shipping providers, and marketing tools to streamline your workflow and enhance the customer experience. Mobile responsiveness ensures that your store looks and functions well on all devices, meeting the needs of customers who shop on their phones and tablets.

Security features are essential to protect your business and customers' data. For payment processing, look for platforms that comply with industry standards, such as PCI-DSS. Scalability is also important; your platform should be able to handle increased traffic and sales as your business grows. Finally, reliable customer support and access to resources, such as tutorials and forums, can make a significant difference in resolving issues and optimizing your store.

Comparing Popular E-commerce Platforms

Several e-commerce platforms stand out for their features, pricing, and ease of use. Shopify is renowned for its simplicity and comprehensive feature set, making it a popular choice for small to medium-sized businesses. WooCommerce offers flexibility and customization, particularly for those familiar with WordPress. Magento is powerful and scalable, ideal for larger enterprises with complex requirements. BigCommerce provides robust built-in features and scalability, while Wix and Squarespace are user-friendly options that cater to smaller businesses and those new to e-commerce.

Each platform has its pros and cons. Shopify, for example, is easy to use but can become expensive with add-ons. WooCommerce offers great flexibility but requires more technical knowledge. Magento is highly customizable and powerful but can be resource-intensive to manage. BigCommerce provides a good balance of features and ease of use, while Wix and Squarespace are excellent for beginners but may lack some advanced functionalities needed by larger businesses.

By understanding these aspects and comparing the top platforms, you can make an informed decision that aligns with your business needs and goals. This chapter will equip you with the knowledge and insights to choose the best e-commerce platform, ensuring a solid foundation for your online store's success.

Setting Up Your E-commerce Platform

Setting up your e-commerce platform is an exciting step in bringing your online store to life. The first thing you need to do is get started with your chosen platform. Most platforms offer a straightforward setup process, guiding you through the initial steps. You'll begin by creating an account and selecting a plan that fits your business needs. Once logged in, the platform's dashboard becomes your command center, where you manage all aspects of your store.

Customizing the design and layout is crucial to making your store stand out and reflect your brand. Most e-commerce platforms come with a variety of themes and templates to choose from. Pick one that resonates with your brand's style and tweak it to make it unique. Adjust colors, fonts, and images to match your brand identity. Customization doesn't stop at aesthetics; you also want to ensure your site is user-friendly. Think about your customer journey and make sure that navigation is intuitive, pages load quickly, and the overall experience is seamless.

Next, you'll start adding products and organizing them into categories. This step is about more than just uploading pictures and descriptions; it's about presenting your products to make it easy for customers to find what they need. Create clear, logical categories and subcategories, and use high-quality images and detailed descriptions to showcase each item. Pay attention to the little details like pricing, SKU numbers, and inventory levels to ensure everything is accurate and up-to-date.

Setting up payment gateways and shipping options is another critical aspect. You want to offer your customers a variety of payment methods to choose from, whether it's credit cards, PayPal, or other digital wallets. This makes the checkout process smoother and builds trust with your customers. Configuring shipping options involves determining your shipping rates and policies. Whether you offer free shipping, flat rates, or calculated shipping based on location, ensure it's clearly communicated to avoid surprises at checkout.

Security settings are paramount for protecting your store and your customers' information. Configuring these settings ensures that your store complies with industry standards and regulations. This includes setting up SSL certificates to encrypt data, enabling two-factor authentication for added security, and regularly updating your software to protect against vulnerabilities. It's also important to familiarize yourself with and comply with regulations like GDPR if you have customers in Europe, ensuring that you handle personal data responsibly and transparently.

In summary, setting up your e-commerce platform involves several key steps: getting started with the platform, customizing your store to reflect your brand, adding and organizing products, setting up payment and shipping options, and configuring security settings. Each of these steps plays a crucial role in creating a professional and efficient online store that meets your business goals and provides a seamless shopping experience for your customers.

Optimizing Your E-commerce Store for Success

Optimizing your e-commerce store for success involves several strategic steps to ensure your business stands out in a competitive market. One of the most crucial aspects is implementing SEO best practices. SEO, or search engine optimization, is about making your store more visible on search engines like Google. By optimizing your product titles, descriptions, and images with relevant keywords, you can drive more organic traffic to your site. This means more potential customers find your products through regular search queries. Creating a blog or content hub with valuable information related to your products can further enhance your SEO efforts, making your site a go-to resource for shoppers.

Creating compelling product descriptions and visuals is another key factor. Your product descriptions should be detailed and engaging, highlighting each item's benefits and unique features. High-quality images are equally important, giving customers a clear and attractive view of what they're buying. Consider using multiple images for each product, showing different angles and uses. Videos can also be incredibly effective, offering a dynamic way to showcase your products in action.

Utilizing analytics is essential for tracking your store's performance and making informed decisions. Tools like Google Analytics can provide insights into how customers are interacting with your site, what products are selling well, and where there might be bottlenecks in the purchasing process. By regularly reviewing this data, you can identify trends and areas for improvement, allowing you to optimize your marketing efforts and product offerings.

Implementing marketing strategies such as email marketing, social media campaigns, and pay-per-click (PPC) advertising can significantly boost your store's visibility and sales. Email marketing keeps your customers engaged with personalized content, special offers, and updates about new products. Social media campaigns allow you to connect with your audience on platforms they frequently use, creating a community around your brand. PPC advertising helps you reach potential customers who are actively searching for products like yours, ensuring that your marketing budget is spent efficiently.

Enhancing user experience is critical to keeping visitors on your site and encouraging them to make a purchase. This includes ensuring easy navigation so customers can quickly find what they're looking for and fast loading times to prevent frustration and drop-offs. A well-designed, intuitive website keeps customers engaged and increases the likelihood of conversion.

Managing and maintaining your e-commerce platform requires ongoing attention and effort. Regular updates to your platform and plugins are necessary for both security and functionality. This helps protect your site from vulnerabilities and ensures that all features work smoothly. Monitoring site performance is also important; promptly resolving issues can prevent small problems from becoming major disruptions.

Efficiently managing inventory and processing orders ensures that your operations run smoothly. Keeping accurate inventory records prevents stockouts and overstock situations, while a streamlined order processing system ensures that customers receive their purchases quickly and accurately.

Providing excellent customer service and effectively handling returns are essential for building trust and loyalty. Ensure your customer service team is responsive and helpful, promptly addressing any issues or questions. A clear and fair return policy can also enhance customer satisfaction, making it easy for them to shop with confidence.

Continuously improving and adapting your store based on feedback and analytics is key to long-term success. Listen to your customers and use their feedback to make improvements. Regularly review your analytics to understand what's working and what's not, and be willing to make changes as needed. This proactive approach ensures that your store remains relevant and competitive in a constantly evolving market.

In summary, optimizing and maintaining your e-commerce store involves a combination of effective SEO practices, compelling content, data-driven decision-making, strategic marketing, and a focus on user experience. By staying attentive to these elements, you can create a thriving online store that attracts and retains customers, driving sustained success for your business.

INTEGRATING ADDITIONAL TOOLS AND SERVICES

Integrating additional tools and services into your e-commerce platform can significantly enhance your business's functionality and efficiency. Adding plugins and extensions is one of the most effective ways to do this. For instance, a customer relationship management (CRM) system can help you keep track of customer interactions, preferences, and purchase history, enabling more personalized marketing and better customer service. An enterprise resource planning (ERP) system can streamline your business processes by integrating various functions like inventory management, order processing, and human resources. Marketing automation tools can simplify and optimize your marketing efforts, from email campaigns to social media management.

Integrating with third-party services is another critical step. You can automate and streamline your logistics operations by connecting your e-commerce platform with fulfillment centers. This integration ensures that orders are processed and shipped quickly, enhancing customer satisfaction. Accounting software integrations help you keep your financials in order by automatically syncing sales data, expenses, and inventory costs, reducing manual data entry and minimizing errors.

Exploring multi-channel selling opportunities can also expand your reach and increase sales. Selling on platforms like Amazon, eBay, and social media shops allows you to tap into larger audiences. Each platform has its own tools and audience demographics, so it's important to tailor your approach for each. For instance, Amazon's marketplace can give you access to millions of potential customers, while social media shops on platforms like Instagram and Facebook allow you to engage directly with your audience through targeted ads and interactive posts.

Incorporating these tools and services requires careful planning and execution. Start by identifying the specific needs of your business and researching the available options. Look for solutions that offer seamless integration with your current e-commerce platform and provide the features you need. Once you've selected the tools and services that will benefit your business, take the time to properly set them up and train your team on how to use them effectively.

Adding these enhancements can create a more efficient, scalable, and customer-friendly operation. These integrations help you automate routine tasks, manage your business more effectively, and reach new customers across multiple channels. This holistic approach improves your current operations and positions your business for future growth and success.

Future Trends in E-commerce Platforms

The future of e-commerce platforms is brimming with exciting possibilities, driven by emerging technologies that promise to revolutionize the way we conduct business online. Artificial intelligence (AI) is at the forefront of this transformation. AI can enhance various aspects of e-commerce, from personalizing shopping experiences to optimizing inventory management. With AI, we can analyze customer behavior in real time, providing personalized product recommendations and dynamic pricing strategies that meet individual preferences and maximize sales.

Augmented reality (AR) is another game-changing technology that is making waves in e-commerce. AR allows customers to visualize products in their own environment before purchasing. For instance, they can see how a piece of furniture would look in their living room or how a pair of shoes would fit. This immersive experience boosts customer confidence and reduces return rates, as customers are more likely to be satisfied with their purchases.

Voice commerce is rapidly gaining traction as well. With the increasing popularity of smart speakers and virtual assistants like Alexa and Google Assistant, more consumers are using voice commands to search for and purchase products online. This hands-free, convenient shopping method is set to become a significant part of the e-commerce landscape, necessitating platforms to optimize for voice search and streamline voice-activated purchase processes.

Personalization and enhancing customer experience continue to be critical trends in e-commerce. Customers now expect tailored experiences that cater to their unique needs and preferences. This means e-commerce platforms must leverage data analytics to offer personalized recommendations, targeted promotions, and customized shopping journeys. Creating a seamless and intuitive user experience across all touchpoints is vital for retaining customers and fostering brand loyalty.

Looking ahead, we can expect e-commerce platforms to evolve in several ways. First, the integration of AI, AR, and voice commerce will become more sophisticated, making online shopping more interactive and engaging. Second, platforms will emphasize omnichannel experiences more, ensuring a consistent and cohesive brand presence across online, mobile, and physical channels. Third, we will see an increased focus on sustainability and ethical practices as consumers become more conscious of the environmental and social impact of their purchases.

The future of e-commerce platforms is shaped by innovative technologies that enhance personalization and customer experience. By staying ahead of these trends and continuously adapting to new advancements, businesses can ensure they remain competitive and meet their customers' evolving expectations. This proactive approach will drive growth and build a loyal customer base that values the convenience and personalized experiences offered by modern e-commerce platforms.

Conclusion

Choosing the right e-commerce platform is a cornerstone of building a successful online business. Throughout this chapter, we've delved into the critical aspects of selecting and using an e-commerce platform. We began by understanding the importance of this choice, which influences every facet of your business operations, from ease of use and customization to integration capabilities and security features.

We discussed the different types of e-commerce platforms, including hosted and self-hosted options, and examined popular choices like Shopify, WooCommerce, and Magento. Each platform has strengths and weaknesses, and the right choice depends on your business needs and goals. We explored key features to look for, such as a user-friendly interface, customization options, integration capabilities, mobile responsiveness, security, scalability, and reliable customer support.

Setting up your e-commerce platform involves more than just choosing the right one. It's about customizing the design to match your brand, adding and organizing products effectively, setting up payment gateways and shipping options, and ensuring robust security settings. These steps lay the foundation for a functional, attractive online store that meets your customers' expectations.

Optimizing your e-commerce store for success requires a focus on SEO best practices, compelling product descriptions, and effective use of analytics to track performance. Implementing strategic marketing campaigns, enhancing user experience, and continuously monitoring and maintaining your platform is essential for staying competitive and ensuring customer satisfaction.

We also covered the importance of integrating additional tools and services to enhance your store's functionality and efficiency. From adding plugins and extensions to integrating with third-party services and exploring multi-channel selling opportunities, these integrations can significantly boost your business operations and reach.

Emerging technologies like AI, AR, and voice commerce are set to transform e-commerce platforms. These advancements will bring new levels of personalization, interactivity, and convenience to online shopping. Staying informed about these trends and incorporating them into your strategy will keep your business ahead of the curve.

In conclusion, selecting the right e-commerce platform is vital for the success of your online business. It impacts every aspect of your operations, from daily management to long-term growth. Continuously evaluating and improving your e-commerce strategy is essential to adapt to changing technologies and customer expectations. By making informed decisions and staying proactive, you can build a thriving online store that attracts and retains customers, driving sustained success in the digital marketplace.

7

INTEGRATING CRM, TECHNOLOGY, AND SUSTAINABILITY IN FULFILLMENT

Integrating Customer Relationship Management (CRM), advanced technology, and sustainability into the fulfillment process is crucial for staying competitive in today's market. Each of these elements plays a vital role in ensuring that our fulfillment operations are efficient and responsive to the evolving demands of our customers and the environment.

CRM systems are indispensable tools that help us understand and engage with our customers more effectively. By leveraging CRM data, we can personalize our interactions, anticipate customer needs, and deliver a more tailored shopping experience. This deepened customer relationship fosters loyalty and repeat business, which are key to long-term success.

Technology, on the other hand, revolutionizes the way we manage our fulfillment operations. Technology enables us to operate more efficiently and make informed decisions, from automated warehousing solutions that streamline inventory management to data analytics that provide insights into customer behavior and market trends. These advancements speed up the fulfillment process and reduce errors, ensuring that our customers receive their orders promptly and accurately.

Sustainability is no longer just a buzzword; it's a critical component of modern business practices. Consumers are increasingly looking for brands that align with their values, and incorporating sustainable practices into our fulfillment process can significantly enhance our brand reputation. This includes everything from using eco-friendly packaging materials to optimizing delivery routes to reduce carbon emissions. By committing to sustainability, we help protect the environment and appeal to a growing base of eco-conscious customers.

In this chapter, we will explore each of these components in detail. We'll start by discussing the role of CRM in fulfillment, including how to choose and implement the right CRM system and the benefits it can bring to our operations. Next, we'll delve into the various technologies that can enhance our fulfillment process, from automation to data analytics, and how to effectively integrate these tools into our existing systems. Finally, we'll examine the importance of sustainability in fulfillment, offering practical steps to adopt eco-friendly practices and the benefits of doing so.

By the end of this chapter, you will have a comprehensive understanding of how CRM, technology, and sustainability intersect to create a robust and successful fulfillment strategy. You'll see how these elements work together to improve efficiency, customer satisfaction, and brand loyalty, positioning your business for sustained growth and success in an increasingly competitive marketplace.

EFFECTIVE CUSTOMER RELATIONSHIP MANAGEMENT (CRM)

Effective Customer Relationship Management (CRM) plays a crucial role in the fulfillment process, ensuring that we understand and meet our customers' needs in a personalized and efficient manner. A good CRM system helps us track and analyze every interaction with our customers, from when they first visit our website to where they receive their orders. This comprehensive understanding of the customer journey allows us to tailor our communications and offerings to better match their preferences and behaviors, ultimately enhancing customer satisfaction.

Choosing the right CRM system is an important step. There are several key features to look for, including user-friendly interfaces, robust data analytics capabilities, and seamless integration with our existing e-commerce platform. Popular CRM systems for e-commerce businesses include Salesforce, HubSpot, and Zoho CRM, each offering unique advantages depending on our specific needs. Salesforce, for example, is known for its powerful customization options and scalability, making it a great choice for growing businesses. HubSpot offers a more intuitive and accessible platform, ideal for smaller businesses or those new to CRM systems. Zoho CRM provides a comprehensive suite of tools that can be tailored to various business requirements.

Implementing a CRM system in our fulfillment process requires careful planning and execution. First, we need to ensure that the CRM system integrates smoothly with our e-commerce platform. This integration allows for real-time data synchronization, ensuring that customer information is always up-to-date and accurate. Training our staff to use the CRM system effectively is equally important. They need to understand how to leverage the system's features to track customer interactions, manage leads, and analyze data. Providing ongoing training and support will help our team stay proficient with the system and use it to its full potential.

The benefits of a well-implemented CRM system in fulfillment are substantial. One of the primary advantages is the ability to provide personalized customer experiences. By analyzing customer data, we can identify patterns and preferences to tailor our marketing messages, product recommendations, and customer service interactions. This level of personalization makes customers feel valued and understood, increasing their loyalty to our brand.

Improved customer service and support are other significant benefits of CRM systems. With a centralized database of customer information, our support team can quickly access past interactions and purchase history, providing faster and more accurate responses to customer inquiries. This not only improves the customer experience but also boosts the efficiency of our support operations.

Finally, a CRM system enables data-driven decision-making. By leveraging the insights gained from customer data, we can make more informed decisions about our marketing strategies, product offerings, and fulfillment processes. This helps us allocate resources more effectively, optimize our operations, and ultimately drive growth.

In summary, effective Customer Relationship Management is a cornerstone of successful fulfillment. By understanding the customer journey, choosing the right CRM system, integrating it with our e-commerce platform, and training our staff, we can provide personalized experiences, improve customer service, and make data-driven decisions that enhance our overall business performance.

LEVERAGING TECHNOLOGY FOR FULFILLMENT

Leveraging technology in fulfillment is essential for maintaining a competitive edge in today's fast-paced market. Staying current with technological advancements is not just a luxury; it's a necessity. The right technology can significantly enhance our efficiency and accuracy, which translates into better customer satisfaction and higher profitability. With the rapid pace of innovation, keeping up with the latest tools and solutions allows us to streamline our operations, reduce costs, and stay ahead of our competitors.

The role of technology in modern fulfillment cannot be overstated. Automated warehousing solutions, for example, revolutionize how we handle inventory. These systems use sophisticated algorithms and robotics to manage storage and retrieval tasks, minimizing human error and speeding up the entire process. Automating these tasks ensures that our inventory is always accurately accounted for and easily accessible, which is crucial for timely order fulfillment.

Robotics and automation play a pivotal role in order processing as well. Automated conveyor systems, robotic pickers, and sorters can handle a high volume of orders with precision and speed that humans simply can't match. This increases our throughput and reduces the risk of errors, ensuring that customers receive the correct items in their orders. Implementing these technologies requires an initial investment, but the return in terms of efficiency and reduced labor costs is substantial.

Data analytics is another critical technology in fulfillment. We can make informed decisions about stock management and demand forecasting by analyzing inventory levels, sales trends, and customer behavior. This helps us maintain optimal inventory levels, reducing both stockouts and excess inventory. Accurate demand forecasting also enables us to plan our purchasing and production schedules more effectively, minimizing waste and maximizing profitability.

Integrating new technologies into our fulfillment process involves several steps. First, we need to assess our current operations and identify areas where technology can make the most significant impact. We can begin the integration process once we've identified the right solutions. This often involves working closely with technology providers to ensure that the new systems are compatible with our existing infrastructure. Training and support for our staff are crucial during this transition. Our team needs to understand how to use the new technologies effectively to maximize their benefits. Providing comprehensive training and ongoing support helps our employees adapt to the changes and feel confident in using the new systems. Managing technological change also involves clear communication and setting realistic expectations. Change can be challenging, but we can ensure a smooth transition with the right approach.

The benefits of leveraging technology in fulfillment are numerous. Enhanced efficiency and productivity mean we can process more orders in less time, directly impacting our bottom line. Reduced errors and faster processing times increase customer satisfaction, as orders are fulfilled accurately and promptly. Better inventory management through data analytics helps us optimize our stock levels, reducing holding costs and minimizing the risk of stockouts. These improvements not only save money but also enhance our overall operational efficiency.

Leveraging technology in fulfillment is essential for staying competitive and meeting the demands of today's market. We can significantly enhance our efficiency, accuracy, and profitability by staying current with technological advancements, implementing key technologies, and effectively managing the integration process. This proactive approach ensures that we can continue to deliver exceptional service to our customers and drive long-term success for our business.

Sustainability in Fulfillment

Sustainability in fulfillment is becoming increasingly important as consumers demand more eco-friendly practices from the businesses they support. This shift in consumer behavior is more than a trend; it's a clear signal that people are prioritizing the health of our planet. Embracing sustainability isn't just about meeting consumer expectations—it's about securing long-term benefits for our business and the environment.

Integrating sustainable practices into our fulfillment process begins with eco-friendly packaging solutions. Traditional packaging materials contribute significantly to waste and pollution. We can reduce our environmental impact by switching to biodegradable, recyclable, or reusable materials. This change might seem small, but it has a considerable effect when multiplied by the thousands of packages we send monthly. Additionally, optimizing the size and shape of our packaging to fit the products better can reduce material usage and lower shipping costs, as smaller, lighter packages are cheaper to transport.

Energy-efficient warehousing is another critical area. Warehouses consume a lot of energy, from lighting and heating to cooling systems and equipment operation. By investing in energy-efficient lighting, such as LED bulbs, and using programmable thermostats, we can significantly cut down on our energy consumption. Implementing solar panels or other renewable energy sources can further enhance our sustainability efforts. These changes reduce our carbon footprint and lead to substantial cost savings over time.

Optimizing transportation and logistics is crucial for reducing emissions. This involves planning delivery routes more efficiently, consolidating shipments to minimize the number of trips, and using fuel-efficient vehicles. Partnering with logistics providers who prioritize sustainability, such as those offering carbon-neutral shipping options, can also make a big difference. Focusing on these areas can reduce our overall environmental impact while maintaining or improving our delivery performance.

Implementing sustainability in our fulfillment process requires a structured approach. The first step is adopting sustainable practices across our operations. This might involve auditing our current practices to identify areas for improvement, setting clear sustainability goals, and developing a plan to achieve them. Engaging and educating our staff is crucial. Everyone in the organization needs to understand the importance of these changes and how they can contribute. Training sessions, workshops, and regular updates can keep sustainability at the forefront of our minds.

Tracking and measuring our sustainability efforts are essential for continuous improvement. We can see what's working and where we need to adjust by setting benchmarks and regularly monitoring our progress. This data helps us stay accountable and provides valuable insights that can drive further innovations.

The benefits of adopting sustainable practices in fulfillment are numerous. Enhancing our brand reputation is one of the most significant advantages. Consumers are more likely to support businesses that align with their values, and demonstrating a commitment to sustainability can differentiate us from competitors. Increased customer loyalty often follows, as customers appreciate and trust companies that take responsibility for their environmental impact.

Cost savings from reduced waste and energy use are another major benefit. While an initial investment might be required to implement sustainable practices, the long-term savings can be substantial. Lower energy bills, reduced material costs, and more efficient operations all contribute to a healthier bottom line.

Integrating sustainability into our fulfillment process is not just a response to growing consumer demand; it's a strategic move that benefits our business and the environment. By adopting eco-friendly packaging, energy-efficient warehousing practices, and optimizing our logistics, we can reduce our environmental impact, enhance our brand reputation, and achieve significant cost savings. Engaging our staff and tracking our progress ensures that these efforts are effective and continuously improving, setting us up for long-term success in a world that increasingly values sustainability.

Integrating CRM, Technology, and Sustainability

Creating a unified fulfillment strategy by integrating CRM, technology, and sustainability is a game-changer for any business looking to enhance its operations. By aligning these elements, we can build a strategy that meets the current market demands and prepares us for future challenges. The key is to ensure that our goals for customer relationship management, technological advancements, and sustainability are seamlessly woven together.

When I think about creating a unified strategy, the first step is aligning our CRM goals with our technology and sustainability objectives. This means ensuring that every part of our fulfillment process works toward the same end. For instance, integrating our CRM with our e-commerce platform allows us to collect and analyze customer data more effectively. This data is invaluable for making informed decisions that support our sustainability goals, such as reducing waste or optimizing our logistics to lower emissions. It's all about creating a cohesive system where each component enhances the others, driving efficiency and customer satisfaction.

One of this integrated approach's biggest advantages is its holistic view. With CRM and technology working hand in hand, we gain a comprehensive understanding of our operations and customer interactions. This transparency improves decision-making, making identifying bottlenecks, forecasting demand, and streamlining our processes easier. Plus, with sustainability practices embedded in our strategy, we're not just focusing on profit but also on reducing our environmental footprint. This holistic view ultimately strengthens our brand, boosting customer loyalty and satisfaction because people appreciate responsible and forward-thinking businesses.

To integrate CRM, technology, and sustainability effectively, I started with a thorough needs assessment and gap analysis. This helped us identify where we stood and what needed to be improved. From there, we developed a comprehensive integration plan. This plan included timelines, responsibilities, and milestones, ensuring everyone was on the same page. Training is crucial, so we invested in workshops and training sessions for our staff across all departments. This wasn't just about teaching them how to use new software or follow new processes—it was about getting them on board with our vision of a more integrated, sustainable, and tech-savvy operation.

Once everything was in place, monitoring and continuous improvement became our focus. We set up regular reviews of our integration strategy, using data and feedback from our customers and staff to drive ongoing improvements. This approach helps us stay adaptable and ready to pivot or adopt new technologies as trends and market demands evolve. Whether it's adopting new CRM features, enhancing our sustainability practices, or upgrading our technology, staying flexible is key to maintaining our competitive edge.

Integrating CRM, technology, and sustainability into our fulfillment strategy has transformed our operations. It has given us a unified approach that enhances our efficiency, boosts our decision-making capabilities, and strengthens our relationship with customers. By continuously reviewing and updating our strategy, we ensure that we stay ahead of the curve, ready to embrace new opportunities and tackle challenges head-on.

This integrated approach drives business growth and fosters a positive impact on the environment and society, creating a win-win situation for everyone involved.

Conclusion

This chapter explored how integrating CRM, technology, and sustainability into our fulfillment process creates a powerful strategy for success. We discussed how a unified approach enhances efficiency, boosts decision-making, and strengthens customer relationships. We can create a cohesive system that benefits our business and the environment by aligning our CRM goals with technological advancements and sustainable practices.

The importance of this integration cannot be overstated. Effective CRM allows us to understand and engage with our customers on a deeper level, providing personalized experiences that build loyalty. Leveraging technology streamlines our operations, reduces errors, and increases productivity, making our processes more efficient and cost-effective. Incorporating sustainability ensures that we are doing our part to protect the environment while also appealing to the growing number of eco-conscious consumers.

As we move forward, it's essential to continuously evaluate and improve our fulfillment practices. The business landscape is always changing, and staying adaptable is key to maintaining our competitive edge. Regularly reviewing our strategies, collecting data, and seeking feedback will help us identify areas for improvement and make informed decisions. Embracing new technologies and sustainable practices as they emerge will keep us ahead of the curve.

Integrating CRM, technology, and sustainability into our fulfillment process is a strategic move that sets us up for long-term success. It allows us to operate more efficiently, make better decisions, and build stronger relationships with our customers. By committing to continuous improvement, we can ensure that our fulfillment practices remain effective, sustainable, and responsive to the needs of our customers and the market. This proactive approach not only drives business growth but also creates a positive impact on the world around us.

8

STRATEGIES FOR GLOBAL EXPANSION

Globally expanding your business is pivotal in achieving substantial growth and long-term success. Entering international markets opens new revenue streams and helps diversify your business, making it more resilient to local economic fluctuations. The potential to tap into new customer bases, enhance brand recognition, and leverage global talent can drive innovation and competitiveness.

However, global expansion is not without its challenges. Navigating different regulatory environments, understanding diverse cultural nuances, and managing logistics across borders require thorough planning and strategic execution. The benefits are significant, but they need careful analysis and adaptation to local markets.

This chapter will explore the various facets of global expansion, starting with market research and analysis to identify the most promising markets for your business. We'll discuss entry strategies, from direct exporting to forming local partnerships, and the importance of adapting your products and services to meet local needs. We will also cover the complexities of supply chain management and logistics, ensuring you can deliver your products efficiently worldwide.

We'll delve into the legal and financial considerations necessary for international operations, such as compliance with local laws and managing foreign exchange risks. Building a global brand requires consistency and adaptability, so we'll discuss strategies for maintaining your brand's integrity while resonating with diverse audiences.

Risk management is crucial, as entering new markets involves various uncertainties. We'll provide insights on identifying potential risks and developing mitigation strategies. Finally, we'll focus on monitoring and evaluation to ensure continuous improvement and long-term success in your global ventures.

By the end of this chapter, you will have a comprehensive understanding of the key areas involved in global expansion and be equipped with strategies to navigate this complex but rewarding journey.

Market Research and Analysis

Identifying the right target markets is the first crucial step in any global expansion strategy. It's not just about finding where there's demand for your product; it's about evaluating a range of criteria to ensure a market is a good fit for your business. Economic stability, growth potential, and consumer purchasing power are essential factors to consider. Additionally, understanding the cultural and political environment is vital. A country with a high demand for your product might still pose significant risks if it has an unstable political climate or regulatory environment.

Understanding local consumer behavior is equally important. Every market has unique cultural nuances that influence buying habits. What sells well in one country might not resonate in another. For example, consumers in some regions might prefer locally sourced products, while others prioritize international brands. Adapting your products and marketing strategies to fit these preferences is crucial. This might involve modifying your product design, adjusting your pricing strategy, or tailoring your advertising messages to align with local values and lifestyles.

Conducting a thorough competitive analysis is also necessary. Identifying local competitors and market leaders helps you understand the competitive landscape. Analyzing their strengths and weaknesses can reveal gaps in the market that your business can exploit. It also helps you learn from their successes and mistakes, allowing you to develop strategies that leverage your unique strengths and address any potential challenges.

Navigating regulatory and legal considerations is another complex but essential aspect of global expansion. Each country has its own laws and regulations governing business operations. These can include labor laws, environmental regulations, and industry-specific standards. Understanding these laws is critical to avoiding legal pitfalls and ensuring smooth operations. Additionally, trade barriers and tariffs can significantly impact your business. Knowing these factors and planning accordingly can help you mitigate risks and avoid unexpected costs.

Thorough market research and analysis are the foundation of successful global expansion. By carefully selecting target markets, understanding local consumer behavior, conducting competitive analysis, and navigating regulatory landscapes, you can make informed decisions that position your business for success in new international markets. This comprehensive approach ensures that you are not only entering markets with high potential but also doing so in a sustainable and profitable way.

Entry Strategies

When considering global expansion, selecting the right entry strategy is essential to navigating new markets effectively. One common approach is direct exporting. This method allows you to sell your products directly to customers in foreign markets without needing a physical presence there. The primary advantage of direct exporting is control. You maintain direct oversight over your brand and product quality, upholding your business standards. However, the main challenge is managing logistics and distribution from a distance, which can be complex and costly. Setting up efficient distribution channels is crucial. This might involve finding reliable local distributors or establishing partnerships with logistics companies that can handle your products' shipping, customs clearance, and delivery.

Partnerships and alliances are another strategic option. Forming partnerships with local businesses can provide invaluable insights and facilitate smoother market entry. Local partners can help you navigate regulatory landscapes, cultural nuances, and consumer preferences more effectively than you could on your own. The key is to find and evaluate potential partners carefully. Look for businesses that complement your own, have a solid market presence, and share your values and business goals. A good partnership can accelerate your market entry and help mitigate risks by leveraging local expertise and resources.

Franchising and licensing offer yet another pathway for expanding into international markets. Franchising involves allowing other business owners to operate under your brand using your business model. This approach can lead to rapid expansion with lower capital investment since franchisees typically bear the costs of opening and operating new locations. On the other hand, licensing involves granting rights to a local business to produce and sell your products. While both models can provide quick market penetration, they also come with challenges. Maintaining consistent brand standards and quality across multiple franchises or licensees can be difficult, and you need to ensure that your intellectual property is adequately protected.

Establishing a local presence is often necessary for businesses seeking a deeper commitment to a new market. This might involve setting up local offices or subsidiaries to manage operations directly. Having a physical presence in the market can enhance credibility, improve customer relationships, and provide better control over operations. Hiring and managing local staff is a critical aspect of this strategy. Employing locals who understand the market dynamics and culture can provide significant advantages. However, it also means navigating local labor laws, building a new team, and creating a management structure that aligns with both your home office and local operations.

In summary, choosing the right entry strategy depends on various factors, including your business goals, resources, and the specific characteristics of the target market. Whether you opt for direct exporting, partnerships, franchising, or establishing a local presence, each approach has its benefits and challenges. Careful planning and thorough research are essential to making an informed decision that aligns with your long-term objectives. By understanding the nuances of each entry strategy and implementing them effectively, you can successfully navigate the complexities of global expansion and build a sustainable presence in new markets.

Adapting Products and Services

Expanding into international markets requires more than just selling the same products and services you offer at home. It often involves significant customization to meet local standards and preferences. Product customization is key to ensuring that what you offer resonates with new customers and complies with local regulations. This could mean modifying the product itself, such as adjusting the ingredients of a food item to suit local tastes or altering the features of a gadget to comply with regional safety standards. It also includes adhering to packaging and labeling requirements, which can vary widely from country to country. For instance, certain markets might require information in multiple languages, specific nutritional details, or unique symbols indicating recyclability or safety.

Pricing strategies also need careful consideration. Setting competitive prices in different markets is not as straightforward as converting your home country's prices to the local currency. It involves understanding the local purchasing power, economic conditions, and consumer expectations. In some regions, customers might be willing to pay a premium for foreign brands, while in others, price sensitivity could mean you need to offer more competitive pricing. Balancing these factors while ensuring profitability is crucial. Additionally, it's important to consider local taxes, tariffs, and shipping costs, which can all impact your final pricing strategy.

Localization of marketing efforts is another critical aspect. Simply translating your marketing materials isn't enough. You need to adapt your messaging to fit the cultural context of each market. This involves understanding local customs, traditions, and values to create advertising that resonates with your target audience. For example, humor that works in one country might fall flat or even offend in another. Similarly, your imagery and symbols should be culturally appropriate and appealing. Effective localization can significantly enhance the effectiveness of your marketing campaigns, helping you build a strong brand presence in new markets.

Advertising and branding efforts must reflect an understanding of local cultural nuances. This means more than just language translation; it involves adapting the entire marketing approach to fit the local context. A successful brand in a new market is one that feels local while maintaining the essence of its global identity. This might involve partnerships with local influencers, creating region-specific social media campaigns, or sponsoring local events that align with your brand values.

Adapting your products and services for global markets is a multifaceted process that involves customization, strategic pricing, and localized marketing. Each of these elements plays a crucial role in ensuring that your offerings are well-received and competitive in new markets. By taking the time to understand and implement these adaptations, you can effectively navigate the complexities of international expansion and build a successful, globally recognized brand.

Supply Chain and Logistics

Creating an effective global supply chain is critical for any business looking to expand internationally. It starts with managing international suppliers and logistics efficiently. When sourcing materials or products from different countries, it's essential to establish strong relationships with reliable suppliers. This involves vetting potential partners thoroughly, negotiating favorable terms, and regularly assessing their performance to ensure consistent quality. The logistics of moving goods across borders can be complex, involving multiple modes of transportation and coordination among various stakeholders. It requires a robust system to track shipments, manage lead times, and handle any issues that arise promptly.

Ensuring reliability and quality across borders is a significant challenge. Different countries have varying standards and regulations, so ensuring that all products meet your company's standards and local requirements is vital. Regular quality checks and audits are necessary to maintain these standards. Having a reliable logistics network is equally important. Delays or disruptions in the supply chain can lead to stockouts or excess inventory, both of which can hurt your bottom line. Therefore, it's crucial to work with logistics providers that have a proven track record of reliability and efficiency.

Effective inventory management in multiple markets requires strategic planning and execution. One key strategy is to balance local stock levels with central warehousing. This involves determining the right amount of inventory to keep in local markets to meet demand without tying up too much capital in stock. Central warehouses can act as hubs, supplying regional markets and reducing the need for large inventories in every location. This approach not only reduces costs but also improves response times and flexibility.

Choosing the right shipping methods is another crucial aspect of global logistics. Different shipping methods may be more suitable depending on the nature of your products and the destinations. Air freight is fast but expensive, while sea freight is cost-effective but slower. Sometimes, a combination of shipping methods is necessary to optimize cost and speed. Working closely with shipping companies to negotiate the best rates and services is essential.

Navigating customs and import/export regulations can be one of the most daunting aspects of international logistics. Each country has its own set of rules and paperwork requirements, and non-compliance can lead to delays, fines, or even confiscation of goods. It's crucial to stay informed about these regulations and ensure that all documentation is accurate and complete. Partnering with customs brokers or using automated customs software can help streamline this process.

Establishing a robust global supply chain and logistics system is foundational for successful international expansion. It involves managing suppliers and logistics efficiently, ensuring quality across borders, and adopting strategic inventory management practices. Choosing the right shipping methods and navigating customs regulations are also essential components. Businesses can build a reliable and efficient supply chain that supports their global operations and drives growth by focusing on these areas.

Legal and Financial Considerations

Navigating international business's legal and financial landscape requires a careful and informed approach. Ensuring compliance with international laws is a top priority. Each country has its own regulations governing business operations, from labor laws to environmental standards. Adhering to these local laws is crucial to avoid legal complications and penalties. Additionally, international regulations such as trade agreements and treaties must be considered. These rules can impact how goods are imported and exported, the tariffs that apply, and the standards products must meet. Protecting intellectual property rights across different jurisdictions is also essential. This involves registering patents, trademarks, and copyrights in each country where you do business to safeguard your innovations and brand identity.

Financial management in the global arena introduces a new set of challenges. Handling foreign exchange and currency risks is a major concern. Fluctuations in exchange rates can significantly impact your bottom line, especially if you're dealing with multiple currencies. Implementing strategies to hedge against these risks, such as forward contracts or currency options, can help stabilize your financial planning. Setting up local banking and payment systems is another critical step. This ensures that you can efficiently handle transactions in the local currency, making it easier for customers to do business with you and for you to manage your cash flow.

Taxation issues are a complex but unavoidable aspect of international business. Each country has its own tax laws and obligations, and understanding these is crucial to maintaining compliance and optimizing your tax liabilities. Local tax laws will dictate how much tax you need to pay on income earned in that country and any value-added taxes or goods and services taxes that apply to your sales. Managing transfer pricing—the prices at which goods and services are sold between your company's subsidiaries in different countries—requires careful attention to ensure compliance with international tax regulations and to avoid double taxation. Effective tax optimization strategies can help you minimize your tax burden while staying within legal requirements, thereby improving your profitability.

Legal and financial considerations play a crucial role in the success of your international operations. Ensuring compliance with both local and international regulations protects your business from legal issues and helps maintain a good reputation. Effective financial management, including handling currency risks and setting up robust payment systems, ensures smooth operations and financial stability. Understanding and managing taxation issues, particularly transfer pricing and tax optimization, helps maximize your profitability while maintaining compliance. By paying close attention to these areas, you can navigate the complexities of global business with confidence and build a solid foundation for long-term success.

BUILDING A GLOBAL BRAND

Building a global brand is both an exciting opportunity and a complex challenge. At the heart of this endeavor is finding the right balance between consistency and adaptability. Maintaining brand consistency across markets is crucial because it ensures that customers recognize and trust your brand no matter where your customers are. This consistency involves everything from your logo and color scheme to your core values and brand voice. It's about creating a unified image that stands for the same principles and quality, no matter the location.

However, while consistency is important, adaptability is equally essential. Each market has its unique cultural nuances, and your brand messaging needs to reflect that. Adapting your brand to local cultures means understanding and respecting these differences. It might involve altering your marketing messages, product names, or certain features to resonate with local consumers better. This adaptation shows that you value and understand your diverse customer base, which can significantly enhance your brand's acceptance and success in new markets.

When it comes to global marketing campaigns, a strategic approach is key. Advertising and promoting your brand on a global scale requires careful planning and execution. It's about choosing the right channels and messages that will reach and resonate with your target audience in each market. Digital marketing plays a crucial role in this. Leveraging social media, search engines, and online advertising allows you to reach international audiences efficiently and effectively. Digital platforms provide powerful tools to segment your audience, tailor your messages, and track the performance of your campaigns in real-time.

Building trust and reputation in new markets is another critical aspect of establishing a global brand. Gaining credibility takes time and consistent effort. You need to deliver on your promises and provide exceptional customer experiences consistently. Good public relations strategies can help you manage your brand's image and reputation. This involves proactive communication, managing media relations, and addressing any issues promptly and transparently. Excellent customer service is also crucial. Providing support in local languages, understanding regional preferences, and responding swiftly to customer inquiries and concerns help build trust and loyalty.

Establishing credibility also means engaging with the local community and contributing positively. This could be through local sponsorships, partnerships, or corporate social responsibility initiatives. Showing that your brand is committed to making a positive impact locally can greatly enhance your reputation and foster strong connections with consumers.

Building a global brand requires a delicate balance of consistency and adaptability. It involves executing well-planned global marketing campaigns and leveraging digital marketing to reach and engage international audiences. Establishing trust and reputation in new markets through excellent public relations and customer service is essential. By focusing on these areas, you can successfully navigate the complexities of global branding and create a strong, respected presence worldwide.

RISK MANAGEMENT

Managing risk is an integral part of expanding globally. As we step into new markets, we must be prepared for a range of potential risks. Political, economic, and cultural factors can all pose significant challenges. Political instability, for example, can disrupt operations and affect market stability. Economic fluctuations can impact everything from consumer purchasing power to currency exchange rates. Cultural differences can lead to misunderstandings or missteps if not properly understood and respected.

Geopolitical events can also have far-reaching impacts. Trade wars, sanctions, and changes in international relations can affect supply chains and market access. It's crucial to stay informed about global developments and understand how they might impact our business. This requires continuous monitoring and analysis of the political and economic landscape in our operating regions.

To mitigate these risks, we need to develop robust strategies. Diversifying our markets and supply chains is one effective approach. We reduce our dependency on any single market or source by spreading our operations across multiple regions and sourcing from various suppliers. This diversification can protect us from localized disruptions and create more stable operations.

Creating contingency plans is another essential part of risk management. We need to anticipate potential disruptions and have plans in place to address them. Whether it's a natural disaster, political unrest, or a sudden economic downturn, having a clear, actionable plan helps us respond quickly and minimize impact. These plans should outline steps to take in various scenarios, ensuring our business can continue operating even under challenging conditions.

Insurance is also a critical component of protecting our international operations. Securing appropriate insurance policies helps safeguard against financial losses due to unforeseen events. This includes coverage for property, liability, and business interruption. Additionally, it's important to protect against operational risks, such as supply chain disruptions or political risks, with specialized insurance products designed for international businesses.

By identifying potential risks, developing mitigation strategies, and securing insurance, we create a safety net that allows us to focus on growth and expansion with confidence. These measures protect our business and provide peace of mind, knowing that we are prepared to handle challenges as they arise. Globally expanding comes with its share of risks, but with careful planning and proactive management, we can navigate these challenges successfully and continue to thrive in the global market.

Monitoring and Evaluation

Monitoring and evaluating our global operations is crucial to ensuring sustained success and growth. To do this effectively,

we need to establish clear performance metrics. Setting key performance indicators (KPIs) tailored to our international markets allows us to measure our progress accurately. These KPIs might include metrics like sales volume, market share, and profitability in each region. By tracking these indicators, we can clearly understand how well we are performing and identify areas that need improvement.

Sales figures give us a direct measure of our market penetration and growth. Monitoring market share helps us understand our competitive position and see how we stack up against local and international competitors. Profitability, meanwhile, tells us whether our operations in each market are financially sustainable. Keeping a close eye on these metrics helps us make informed decisions and adjust our strategies as needed.

Continuous improvement is another critical aspect of monitoring and evaluation. Gathering feedback from local markets is invaluable. This feedback comes from customers, employees, and local partners. By listening to their insights, we can understand what is working and what isn't. This process allows us to adapt our strategies based on real-world performance data. For example, if a particular product isn't resonating with customers in one market, we can tweak it to better meet their needs or adjust our marketing approach.

Adapting strategies based on performance data ensures that we remain agile and responsive. The global market is dynamic, and what works today might not work tomorrow. Being willing to pivot and make changes based on data and feedback keeps us ahead of the curve and positions us for continued success.

Long-term planning is essential for scaling operations and ensuring future growth. Once we have a firm grasp on our current performance, we can start planning how to scale our operations. This might involve expanding our product lines, entering new markets, or investing in new technologies that improve efficiency and customer experience. Scaling operations requires careful planning to ensure that we can meet increased demand without compromising quality or service.

Investing in new markets and technologies is a forward-looking approach that prepares us for future opportunities. Identifying emerging markets with high growth potential allows us to stay ahead of competitors and capture new customer segments. At the same time, investing in technologies like automation, data analytics, and AI can streamline our operations and enhance our decision-making capabilities.

Monitoring and evaluation are ongoing processes that are vital for the success of our global operations. By setting and tracking KPIs, we can measure our performance accurately. Continuous improvement, driven by feedback and performance data, ensures that we remain responsive to market changes. Long-term planning and strategic investments position us for future growth. Through diligent monitoring and proactive adaptation, we can navigate the complexities of the global market and achieve sustained success.

CONCLUSION

Globally expanding is a significant milestone for any business, and this chapter has delved into the essential aspects of making that leap successfully. We've covered the importance of conducting thorough market research and analysis to identify promising markets and understand local consumer behavior. We've looked at various entry strategies, such as direct exporting, partnerships, and establishing a local presence, and how to adapt products and services to meet local preferences.

We also examined the complexities of setting up a global supply chain, from managing international suppliers and logistics to balancing inventory across multiple markets. Understanding the legal and financial considerations, including compliance with local laws, handling currency risks, and optimizing tax strategies, is crucial to operating smoothly in foreign markets. Building a global brand requires consistency while adapting to local cultures and effectively marketing to diverse audiences.

Risk management is vital to navigating the uncertainties of global expansion. Identifying potential risks, developing mitigation strategies, and securing appropriate insurance are necessary steps to protect your business. Finally, monitoring and evaluating your global operations through performance metrics, continuous improvement, and long-term planning ensures that your business remains competitive and grows sustainably.

A strategic approach to global expansion is not just beneficial; it's essential. Every market is different, and understanding these differences while maintaining a cohesive strategy is key to success. The world of international business is full of opportunities, but it also presents unique challenges that require careful planning and execution.

As we move forward, it's important to continuously evaluate and adapt our strategies. The global market is dynamic, and staying flexible and responsive to changes will keep us ahead of the competition. By embracing this mindset, we can navigate the complexities of global expansion, seize new opportunities, and ensure sustained success for our business. This journey requires dedication, but the rewards of establishing a strong global presence are well worth the effort.

9

CONTINUOUS IMPROVEMENT THROUGH CUSTOMER FEEDBACK

Customer feedback is a vital ingredient for the growth and development of any business. Listening to our customers gives us insight into what we're doing right and where we need to improve. It's not just about fixing problems; it's about understanding our customers' evolving needs and preferences. This feedback loop helps us stay relevant and competitive in a constantly changing market.

When we tap into the wealth of information provided by our customers, we can drive continuous improvement across all aspects of our business. Feedback allows us to make informed decisions based on real-world experiences rather than assumptions. Whether it's tweaking a product feature, improving customer service, or streamlining processes, feedback provides the roadmap for making those changes effectively.

In this chapter, we'll explore the different types of customer feedback, how to gather and analyze it, and how to implement changes based on the insights we gain. We'll also look at how feedback contributes to creating a customer-centric culture within our organization.

UNDERSTANDING CUSTOMER FEEDBACK

Customer feedback comes in various forms, each offering unique insights into our business. Direct feedback is the most straightforward and includes surveys, reviews, and feedback forms. These methods allow customers to share their thoughts and experiences directly with us. For example, a post-purchase survey can reveal how satisfied customers are with their buying experience and highlight areas where we can improve.

Indirect feedback is equally important but requires a bit more digging. This includes insights gathered from social media, online forums, and observing customer behavior. Comments and discussions about our brand on social media can reveal trends and sentiments that we might miss through direct feedback alone. Analyzing how customers interact with our website or products can provide valuable clues about their preferences and pain points.

The importance of customer feedback cannot be overstated. Enhancing customer satisfaction and loyalty is perhaps the most immediate benefit. When customers see that their feedback leads to tangible improvements, they feel valued and are more likely to stick with our brand. This loyalty translates into repeat business and positive word-of-mouth recommendations, which are invaluable for growth.

Feedback also helps us identify areas for improvement. No matter how well we think we know our business, there are always blind spots that only customers can reveal. Maybe there's a feature they find confusing or a service aspect that needs refining. We can enhance the overall customer experience and streamline our operations by addressing these issues.

Innovation is another significant benefit of customer feedback. By understanding what our customers want, we can develop new products or services that meet their needs. This customer-driven innovation ensures that we're not just keeping up with the market but setting new trends and standards. For instance, if multiple customers suggest a feature that none of our competitors offer, adding it could give us a unique selling point.

In the following sections, we'll delve deeper into how we can systematically collect, analyze, and act on customer feedback. We'll look at various methods for gathering feedback, the tools and technologies that can help us manage it, and the best practices for ensuring that we use this feedback effectively. By the end of this chapter, you'll clearly understand how to leverage customer feedback to drive continuous improvement and foster a customer-centric culture within your business.

Collecting Customer Feedback

Collecting customer feedback is crucial in understanding how well we meet our customers' needs and expectations. To do this effectively, we need to employ a variety of methods. Surveys and questionnaires are a staple in feedback collection. They allow us to ask specific questions about our products, services, and overall customer experience. A well-designed survey can provide detailed insights into what we are doing right and where we need to improve.

Customer reviews and ratings are another valuable source of feedback. These are often unsolicited and can be found on various platforms, including our website, third-party review sites, and social media. Reviews provide honest and direct customer opinions, highlighting strengths and weaknesses. Regularly monitoring these reviews can help us identify and address recurring issues promptly.

Social media monitoring is also essential. Social media platforms are where customers freely share their experiences and opinions. We can gauge public sentiment and spot emerging trends or problems by keeping an eye on these conversations. This method provides a real-time snapshot of how our brand is perceived and allows us to respond quickly to any negative feedback.

Focus groups and interviews offer a more in-depth approach to collecting feedback. These methods involve engaging directly with a select group of customers to gain deeper insights into their thoughts and feelings. Focus groups can reveal the underlying reasons behind customer preferences and behaviors, while interviews can provide detailed, qualitative data that is hard to capture through surveys alone.

We can leverage various tools and technologies to manage and organize the feedback we collect. Customer feedback software allows us to gather, analyze, and act on feedback from multiple sources in one place. These platforms can automate the collection process, making tracking and responding to feedback in real-time easier. Social listening tools help us monitor and analyze conversations on social media, providing valuable insights into public opinion and trends. Additionally, CRM systems with feedback integration can help us maintain a comprehensive view of our customer interactions, ensuring that we don't miss any critical feedback.

When collecting feedback, it's important to follow best practices to ensure the data we gather is useful and actionable. Asking the right questions is crucial. Our questions should be clear, concise, and focused on specific areas we want to improve. Timing and frequency are also important. Collecting feedback too frequently can overwhelm customers, while collecting it too infrequently can result in missing important insights. Ensuring anonymity and confidentiality encourages more honest and open responses, as customers are more likely to share their true opinions if they feel their privacy is protected.

Analyzing Customer Feedback

Once we have collected feedback, we analyze it. Understanding the difference between quantitative and qualitative feedback is key. Quantitative feedback involves numerical data, such as ratings and survey responses, that can be measured and analyzed statistically. This type of feedback helps us identify trends and patterns in customer behavior and satisfaction. Qualitative feedback, on the other hand, consists of descriptive data, such as comments and interview responses. This feedback provides deeper insights into the reasons behind customer opinions and behaviors.

Using data analytics tools can significantly enhance our ability to analyze feedback. These tools help us identify trends and patterns that might not be immediately apparent. For instance, we can track changes in customer satisfaction over time or compare feedback across different customer segments. Segmenting data allows us to dive deeper into specific areas, understanding how different groups of customers perceive our products and services.

Interpreting feedback is about extracting actionable insights. Knowing what customers think is not enough; we need to understand why they think that way and how we can address their concerns. Prioritizing feedback based on impact and feasibility is crucial. We should focus on the issues that will have the most significant positive effect on customer satisfaction and be realistic about implementing them.

Collecting and analyzing customer feedback involves a systematic approach that combines various methods and tools. By following best practices and leveraging technology, we can gain valuable insights that drive continuous improvement. Understanding and acting on this feedback helps us enhance customer satisfaction, build loyalty, and foster innovation, ensuring our business remains competitive and responsive to our customers' needs.

IMPLEMENTING CHANGES BASED ON FEEDBACK

Putting customer feedback into action starts with developing a solid action plan. It's not enough to just collect and analyze feedback; we need to translate those insights into tangible improvements. Setting clear goals and objectives is the first step. These goals should be specific, measurable, and aligned with our overall business strategy. For instance, if feedback indicates a recurring issue with product quality, our goal might be to reduce defect rates by a certain percentage within a set timeframe.

Next, we need to allocate resources and responsibilities. This means assigning tasks to the right teams and ensuring they have the tools and support they need to succeed. It might involve investing in new equipment, providing additional training for staff, or bringing in external expertise. Clear communication is essential here so everyone understands their role and what is expected of them.

Creating a timeline for implementation helps keep us on track. This timeline should outline key milestones and deadlines, allowing us to monitor progress and adjust as needed. A well-defined plan ensures we stay focused and can measure our progress effectively.

Making operational changes based on feedback is where the rubber meets the road. Process improvements might involve streamlining workflows, adopting new technologies, or revising standard operating procedures to eliminate inefficiencies. Enhancing our products and services based on customer suggestions can lead to higher satisfaction and loyalty. This might mean adding new features, improving existing ones, or addressing common complaints to ensure a better customer experience.

Improving customer service is often a critical area of focus. This can involve training our staff to handle inquiries and issues more effectively, implementing better customer support systems, or extending our service hours to be more accessible to customers. We can build stronger relationships and foster greater loyalty by addressing the feedback we receive about our customer service.

Communicating changes to our customers is a crucial step in this process. Transparency is key. Informing customers about our changes based on their feedback shows that we value their input and are committed to improving their experience. Highlighting the specific improvements and their benefits helps customers see the tangible impact of their feedback. Encouraging further feedback keeps the dialogue open and reinforces the idea that we continuously strive to improve.

Measuring the Impact of Changes

Once changes are implemented, measuring their impact is essential to ensure that they are delivering the desired results. Tracking performance metrics is a critical part of this process. We need to set key performance indicators (KPIs) that align with our goals. These might include metrics like customer satisfaction scores, Net Promoter Scores (NPS), or customer retention rates. By monitoring these KPIs, we can gauge the effectiveness of our changes.

Evaluating how these changes impact our sales and revenue is important. Increased customer satisfaction and loyalty should translate into better financial performance. By comparing sales data before and after implementing changes, we can assess the economic impact of our efforts.

Post-implementation feedback is vital for understanding how well the changes have been received. Collecting this feedback through surveys, reviews, and direct customer interactions allows us to identify any remaining issues or new areas for improvement. This feedback forms a continuous loop, driving ongoing improvement and ensuring that we remain responsive to our customers' needs.

Implementing changes based on customer feedback involves a systematic approach that includes developing an action plan, making operational changes, and communicating with customers. Measuring the impact of these changes ensures that we are on the right track and allows us to make further adjustments as needed. By fostering a culture of continuous improvement driven by customer feedback, we can enhance customer satisfaction, build loyalty, and achieve sustained success.

BUILDING A CUSTOMER-CENTRIC CULTURE

Creating a customer-centric culture is about making the customer the focal point of all our business activities. This begins with fostering an environment where feedback is welcomed, actively sought out, and valued. It's essential to encourage every employee to understand the importance of customer feedback and how it can drive our business forward. We can achieve this through comprehensive training programs that emphasize the significance of listening to customers and acting on their insights. When everyone in the organization understands the value of feedback, it becomes a natural part of our daily operations.

Empowering employees is a crucial aspect of building this culture. This means providing them with the tools and authority they need to respond to customer feedback effectively. Whether it's a front-line employee addressing a customer complaint or a product manager making improvements based on user feedback, everyone should feel empowered to make a difference. Recognizing and rewarding customer-focused initiatives reinforces this behavior. Celebrating successes, whether big or small, helps to embed a customer-centric mindset within the organization. When employees see that their efforts to improve customer satisfaction are acknowledged and rewarded, they are more likely to continue striving for excellence.

Sustaining continuous improvement requires making customer feedback a core part of our business strategy. It's not a one-time effort but an ongoing commitment to listening, learning, and evolving based on what our customers tell us. Regularly reviewing and updating our feedback processes ensures we always capture the most relevant and actionable insights. This might involve using new tools and technologies to gather feedback more effectively or adjusting our survey questions to focus on emerging trends and issues.

Commitment to long-term improvement is what ultimately defines a customer-centric culture. This means setting clear goals for customer satisfaction and continuously measuring our progress against these goals. It's about being proactive rather than reactive—anticipating and addressing customer needs before they become issues. By continuously improving based on customer feedback, we demonstrate our dedication to providing the best possible experience.

Building a customer-centric culture involves creating a feedback-friendly environment, empowering employees, and committing to continuous improvement. By integrating these principles into our everyday operations, we can ensure that our customers always come first. This enhances customer satisfaction and loyalty and drives our business toward greater success. When everyone in the organization is aligned with the goal of putting the customer at the center of everything we do, we create a powerful force for positive change and sustainable growth.

Conclusion

In this chapter, we have explored the critical role of customer feedback in driving continuous improvement within a business. We've discussed various methods for collecting feedback, including surveys, reviews, social media monitoring, and focus groups. We also highlighted the importance of using tools and technologies to streamline the feedback collection process and ensure that we gather actionable insights efficiently.

Analyzing feedback is just as important as collecting it. By understanding the difference between quantitative and qualitative feedback, leveraging data analytics, and interpreting the results, we can extract valuable insights that guide our decision-making process. Implementing changes based on this feedback involves setting clear goals, allocating resources, and communicating effectively with our team and customers. Measuring the impact of these changes ensures that we remain on the right track and allows us to make further adjustments as needed.

The cornerstone of these efforts is building a customer-centric culture. This involves fostering an environment where feedback is valued, empowering employees to act on customer insights, and committing to continuous improvement. When we make customer feedback a core part of our business strategy, we can better understand our customers' needs and expectations, enhancing satisfaction and loyalty.

Customer feedback is not just a tool for identifying problems; it is a powerful resource for fostering innovation and maintaining a competitive edge. By listening to our customers and acting on their insights, we can continuously refine our products, services, and processes, ensuring that we meet and exceed their expectations. This ongoing commitment to improvement helps build strong, lasting relationships with our customers, which are essential for long-term success.

In closing, I encourage you to create a feedback-driven culture within your organization. Make customer feedback an integral part of your business strategy, and prioritize continuous improvement based on the insights you gather. By doing so, you will not only enhance customer satisfaction and loyalty but also drive your business toward greater success. Remember, the key to sustained growth and competitiveness lies in understanding and responding to the voices of those who matter most—your customers.

CONCLUSION

As we reach the conclusion of this book, it's crucial to reflect on the fundamental principles that have been covered. Each chapter has provided a detailed roadmap for improving your fulfillment processes and overall business operations.

SETTING EXPECTATIONS IN FULFILLMENT

One of the foundational aspects of effective fulfillment is setting clear expectations with your customers. This begins with transparent communication about what they can expect from your products and services. Establishing internal processes and standards ensures that everyone within your organization is aligned and understands their role in meeting these expectations. Proactively handling delays and issues is equally important. Customers appreciate honesty and timely updates, which helps maintain trust even when things don't go as planned.

SOURCING QUALITY PRODUCTS

The quality of your products is directly tied to the reliability of your suppliers. Identifying reliable suppliers who can consistently deliver high-quality goods is essential. Negotiating contracts that ensure ethical practices is good for business and enhances your brand's reputation. Implementing strict quality control measures ensures that the products you deliver meet the high standards you've promised your customers.

INVENTORY MANAGEMENT FOR PHYSICAL GOODS

Effective inventory management is critical to meeting customer demand without overstocking or running out of products. Techniques such as just-in-time inventory and safety stock levels help manage inventory efficiently. Leveraging technology for inventory control and optimization allows for real-time tracking and better decision-making. Balancing inventory levels is key to maintaining operational efficiency and ensuring customer satisfaction.

WAREHOUSING AND LOGISTICS

Designing efficient warehouse layouts is about optimizing space and workflow to streamline operations. Leveraging technology in warehousing and logistics, such as automated systems and real-time tracking, can significantly enhance efficiency. Overcoming challenges in physical goods fulfillment often involves addressing issues like delayed shipments or inaccurate order fulfillment, which can be mitigated through better processes and technology.

FULFILLMENT OF DIGITAL GOODS

Digital goods require robust delivery systems to ensure instant and reliable access for customers. Security is paramount to protect digital products from piracy and unauthorized access. Strong customer support for digital products helps address any issues users face. Marketing and legal considerations also play a vital role in the successful fulfillment of digital goods, ensuring compliance with various regulations and effectively reaching target audiences.

CHOOSING AND USING E-COMMERCE PLATFORMS

Selecting the right e-commerce platform is crucial for business success. Key features to look for include ease of use, scalability, and integration capabilities. Setting up and optimizing your online store involves creating a seamless shopping experience for customers. Integrating additional tools and services, such as CRM and marketing automation, can further enhance the functionality of your platform.

INTEGRATING CRM, TECHNOLOGY, AND SUSTAINABILITY IN FULFILLMENT

Leveraging Customer Relationship Management (CRM) systems helps build stronger customer relationships by providing personalized experiences and timely support. Using technology to enhance fulfillment processes, from automated warehousing to data analytics, improves efficiency and accuracy. Implementing sustainable practices in fulfillment benefits the environment and appeals to the growing segment of eco-conscious consumers.

STRATEGIES FOR GLOBAL EXPANSION

Globally expanding requires thorough market research and analysis to understand local markets. Entry strategies must be tailored to each market, considering cultural, economic, and regulatory factors. Managing the supply chain and navigating legal considerations are essential for successful international operations.

CONTINUOUS IMPROVEMENT THROUGH CUSTOMER FEEDBACK

Collecting and analyzing customer feedback is an ongoing process that drives continuous improvement. Implementing changes based on feedback ensures that your business evolves in line with customer expectations. Building a customer-centric culture where feedback is valued and acted upon fosters loyalty and enhances customer satisfaction.

THE FUTURE OF FULFILLMENT IN BUSINESS

The future of fulfillment in business is shaped by emerging technologies, evolving customer expectations, and the need for sustainable practices. Automation, artificial intelligence, and machine learning will continue transforming how businesses operate, making processes more efficient and reducing human error. Customers will increasingly demand faster, more reliable delivery options and greater transparency in the sourcing and production of goods. As businesses respond to environmental concerns and regulatory pressures, sustainable practices will not only become a competitive advantage but a necessity.

FINAL THOUGHTS

As we conclude, it's clear that a strategic approach to fulfillment is essential for business success. The principles and strategies discussed in this book provide a comprehensive framework for enhancing your operations, satisfying your customers, and driving growth. Continuous evaluation and adaptation are crucial. The business landscape is always changing, and staying agile will help you navigate new challenges and seize opportunities.

I encourage you to embrace a feedback-driven culture. Make customer insights a cornerstone of your strategy and commit to continuous improvement. By doing so, you will not only meet but exceed customer expectations, building a loyal customer base and a resilient, successful business. The journey of fulfillment is ongoing, and the efforts you invest in today will pave the way for sustained success in the future.

Work Less and Make More Money Than Ever Before

Take your business to the next level
with a fresh perspective.

These insights show you exactly how to break
through plateaus and achieve big profits.

Go beyond your expectations and
see what's possible for your business.

jetlaunch.link/sab2

www.ingramcontent.com/pod-product-compliance
Lightning Source LLC
Chambersburg PA
CBHW031400180326
41458CB00043B/6549/J